Acquisition.com Volume I

$100M Offers

How To Make Offers So Good People Feel Stupid Saying No

Alex Hormozi

What Others Have Said

"**After spending one day with Alex, we added $5 MILLION PER YEAR in profit** without adding *any* new services. When Alex talks about acquisition, you should listen (as long as you don't hate money)."

— *Brooke Castillo, CEO, Life Coach School*

"My career can be broken into two chapters: the first was 15 years of banging my head against the wall trying to figure out why I was not fulfilling my potential. The second chapter started when I read '$100M Offers' by Alex hormozi. It was then that I had the confidence to know exactly how to have the success that I knew I was capable of enjoying. If you are a business owner that is done settling for less than your potential, this book will quickly show you that it's not your fault; no one has taught you how to make irresistible offers. **This book will change that within a few chapters**. Consider this book your second chapter. **It is an absolute game changer**."

— *Ryan Daniel Moran Founder, Capitalism.com*

"We first found out about Alex and instantly bought his book. It's the best book I've ever read really in business. Probably the biggest thing I learned from him is that so many times in business you want to charge your customers more and you almost feel guilty like 'oh my gosh can I really do this?' but I think there's nobody better that really puts packages and prices together that not only you can increase your price for your business but you're also increasing the value for the customer at the exact same time. **Since we started working with him...within two months...our business was already doing $10M/yr in sales...INSTANT DOUBLE and it's only been two months since we came in touch with him and our business is on a run rate to do $23M/yr in sales now**. Just from changing our pricing, our packaging, and at the same time delivering better results and outcomes for the clients that we work with."

— Andrew Argue *Founder, CEO Accountingtax.com*

Acquisition.com Volume I

$100M Offers

How To Make Offers So Good People Feel Stupid Saying No

By

Alex Hormozi

Print ISBN: 978-1-7374757-3-6

Acquisition.com, LLC

3610-2 N Josey Lane #223

Carrollton,TX 75007-3150

Cover Design by Charlotte Chan Mikkelsen

Photography, Illustrations, and Interior Layout by Alex Hormozi

Guiding Principles

There are no rules.

Thank You

To Leila:

You are my ride-or-die:
a term used to describe a person (usually a woman) that is willing to do anything for their partner, friend, or family, even in the face of danger.
Couldn't do this without you . . . and wouldn't want to.
You make waking up everyday worth it.
Thank you for being unapologetically you.
You're a down motherfucker.

To Trevor:

You're the best friend a guy could ask for.
Thank you for spending hours upon hours beating up the ideas that became this book with me.
It would not be half as good as it is without your relentless drive for simplification and clarity.
Eternally grateful for our friendship.
You make me feel less alone in the world.
Cheers to becoming old and crotchety.

Contents

Start Here 1

SECTION I: How We Got Here **5**

How We Got Here 6

Grand Slam Offers 14

SECTION II: Pricing **22**

Pricing: The Commodity Problem 23

Pricing: Finding The Right Market -- A Starving Crowd 32

Pricing: Charge What It's Worth 43

SECTION III: Value - Create Your Offer **54**

Value Offer: The Value Equation 55

Free Goodwill 69

Value Offer: The Thought Process 71

Value Offer: Creating Your Grand Slam Offer Part I: Problems & Solutions 75

Value Offer: Creating Your Grand Slam Offer Part II: Trim & Stack 83

SECTION IV: Enhancing Your Offer **96**

Enhancing The Offer: Scarcity, Urgency, Bonuses, Guarantees, and Naming 97

Enhancing The Offer: Scarcity 104

Enhancing The Offer: Urgency 112

Enhancing The Offer: Bonuses 117

Enhancing The Offer: Guarantees 124

Enhancing The Offer: Naming 137

SECTION V: Execution **148**

Your First $100,000 149

Start Here

"Outsized returns often come from betting against conventional wisdom, and conventional wisdom is usually right. Given a 10 percent chance of a 100 times payoff, you should take that bet every time. But you're still going to be wrong nine times out of ten . . . We all know that if you swing for the fences, you're going to strike out a lot, but you're also going to hit some home runs. The difference between baseball and business, however, is that baseball has a truncated outcome distribution. When you swing, no matter how well you connect with the ball, the most runs you can get is four. In business, every once in a while, when you step up to the plate, you can score 1,000 runs. This long-tailed distribution of returns is why it's important to be bold. Big winners pay for so many experiments."

— Jeff Bezos

A s entrepreneurs, we make bets everyday. We are gamblers — gambling our hard-earned money on labor, inventory, rent, marketing, etc., all with the hopes of a higher pay out. Oftentimes, we lose. But, sometimes, we win and win BIG. However, there is a difference between gambling in business and gambling in a casino. In a casino, the odds are stacked against you. With skill, you can improve them, but never beat them. In contrast, in business, you can improve your skills to shift the odds *in your favor*. Simply stated, with enough skill, you can become the house.

After beginning a series of books on acquisition, it became apparent that I could not talk about any other topic without first addressing *the offer*: the starting point of any conversation to initiate a transaction with a customer. What you are literally *providing* them in exchange for their money. That's where it all begins.

This book is about how to make profitable offers. Specifically, how to *reliably* turn advertising dollars into (enormous) profits using a combination of pricing, value, guarantees, and naming strategies. I call the proper combination of these components: a *Grand Slam Offer.*

I chose this term partially in homage to the above quote from Amazon founder Jeff Bezos and because, like a grand slam in baseball, a Grand Slam Offer is both very good and very rare. Additionally, to extend the baseball metaphor, it takes no more effort to make a Grand Slam Offer than to strike out. The difference is dictated by the skill of the marketer and how well he connects his offer with his audience's desires. In business you can have so-so offers: the "singles" and "doubles' that keep the game going, pay the bills, and keep the lights on. But, unlike baseball, where a grand slam scores a maximum of four runs, a Grand Slam Offer in the business world, can score you a thousand-fold pay off and result in a world where you never need to work again. It would be like connecting with the ball so well during one single at bat that you automatically win every World Series for the next hundred years.

It takes years of practice to make something as complicated as hitting a major league fastball into the bleachers look effortless. Your stance, vision, prediction, ball speed, bat speed, and hip placement all must be perfect. In marketing and customer acquisition (the process of getting new clients), there are just as many variables that must all align to truly "knock it out of the park." But with enough practice and enough skill, you can turn the wild world of acquisition, which *will* throw curveballs at you everyday, into a homerun derby, knocking offer after offer out of the stadium. To everyone else, your success will look unbelievable. But to you, it will feel like "just another day at work." The greatest hitters of all time also have many strike outs, just as there are many failed offers in the track record of great marketers. We learn skills through failure and practice. We do this knowing that nine out of ten times we will be wrong. We still act boldly, hoping for that offer we connect with so well that it results in our big payoff.

The good news is that in business, you only need to hit *one* Grand Slam Offer to retire forever. I have done this four or five times in my life. As for my track record, I have a 36:1 lifetime return on my advertising dollars over my business career. Consider this my lifetime "batting average," if you will. That means for every $1 I spend on advertising I get $36 back, a 3600% return. That is my *average* over eight years. And I continue to improve.

This book is my attempt to share that skill with you, with a specific focus on building Grand Slam Offers, so you can experience the same levels of success. It's also the first in a series of books meant to get entrepreneurs to financial freedom, in plain words, "fuck you" money. Subsequent books in this series will look more deeply at getting more customers, converting more prospects into clients, making those clients worth more, and other lessons I wish I had learned earlier scaling my businesses.

Pro Tip: Faster, Deeper Learning By Reading & Listening At Same Time

Here's a life hack I discovered a long time ago….If you listen to the audiobook while reading the ebook or physical book you will increase your reading speed and retain more information. The contents are being stored in more places in your brain. This is how I read most things worth reading. I've priced my products as cheap as the platforms will allow me to, so this isn't a ploy to make an extra .99 cents - promise. If you want to give it a try, go ahead and grab the audio version and see for yourself. You might find it as valuable as I have (as someone who struggles to stay focused). I took two days to talk this book out loud and record it. I figured I'd put this "hack" at the beginning of the book so you had a chance to do it if you found this first chapter valuable enough to earn your attention.

SECTION I
How We Got Here

The Ugly Truth

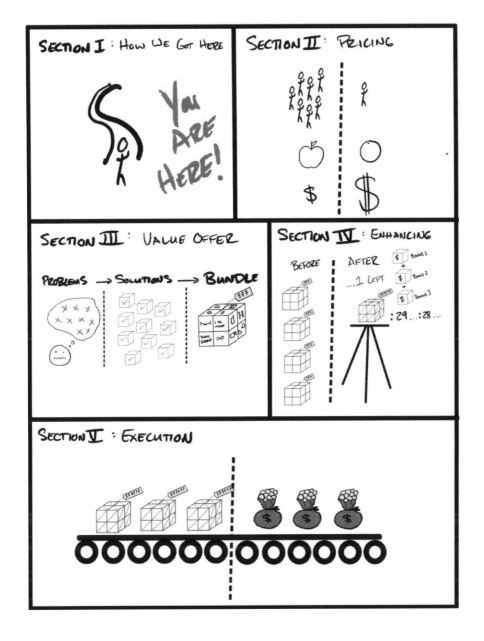

How We Got Here

"Magic will find those with pure hearts, even when all seems lost."

- Morgan Rhodes

December 24, 2016. Christmas Eve.

The room was pitch black. My shoes stuck to a floor covered in dried soda and crushed bits of candy. My nostrils were full with the smell of stale popcorn. We had showed up too late to get good seats and ended up pressed near the front of the theater. Just a few rows in front of me, the movie's blazing projection occupied my entire field of view. In the reflected glow, I could see the outlines of Leila's family's faces. They may as well have been hypnotized.

I envied them. They sat, entranced, soaking in their paid time off for Christmas. *Must be nice.*

Anybody else would have missed it but Leila, my girlfriend at the time, knew me too well. Anybody else would have thought I was watching the movie, but Leila could tell I was staring blankly at the screen, my eyes not tracking the movie. My face was pale. My cheekbones and jawline appeared gaunt. Weeks of chronic stress had killed my appetite.

"What's wrong?" she asked.

I didn't answer.

She rested her hand on mine to get my attention. I didn't react. Within moments, her fingers tightened around my wrist, and she looked at me, her eyes searching for mine. "Your heart is racing," she whispered, concerned.

Without asking, she took my pulse.

It was 100 beats per minute. Nearly twice what it should be for a fit 27 year old male at "rest" in a cool, dark room.

"What's going on?" she asked more forcibly, but still whispering.

The truth is, I was terrified.

A few hours earlier . . .

I looked like a giant. I sat scrunched up in a children's miniature play chair. My knees almost touched my chest, even with my feet firmly planted on the old beige carpeted floor. My laptop felt hot sitting atop my steeply angled knees. Dolls and toys were scattered around me. They stared at me with wide eyes and toothy grins, motionless. I had been their entertainment the past few weeks.

I was in Leila's parents' house. They had recently become grandparents and used this spare bedroom as a playroom when the grandchildren visited. I didn't have a place to live. So they were letting Leila and I stay there "as long as we needed." They had let me use the children's playroom as my office for my "business", which at this point felt almost as make-believe as the stories they had told their grandchildren in this room.

I literally felt like I was playing dress up. Except the stakes were real. And this was my life.

My ears were hot and red from the phone being pressed against them for what felt like hours. I kept switching hands because my arms would tire from holding the phone up for so long.

"I'm sorry Mr. Hormozi," the voice on the other end of the line said, "we have to hold onto these funds for the next six months. We've seen some irregular activity, so this is precautionary."

"Are you fucking kidding me, $120-grand," I said. "A 'precaution'!?"

"I'm sorry sir, our underwriting team—"

"Yeah, I heard you," I said, cutting him off. "I don't accept that."

"Sir, it's not up to me it's just our pol—"

"What am I gonna tell my salesman, who has a baby and another on the way? Are you going to tell him he's not going to be able to buy his pregnant wife and newborn food? Are you going to pay his mortgage for him?"

I was seething.

"Sir—" he began again, with unphased apathy, just trying to deliver the news.

"It's not yours to take." My aggression was quickly turning into desperation. "Shit, just send me half so I can pay my employees," I pleaded "It's Christmas Eve for fuck's sake."

"Sir, we're going to be holding onto the entirety of your funds for the next six months per your agreement . . ." The voice faded into the distance.

Fuck.

I hung up and checked my accounts. *$23,036.*

I owed my salesman a $22,000 commission check for $120,000 in sales I never got. Without wanting to give myself the opportunity to think about it, I wired it to him.

-$22,000 Payment Successful.

Balance $1,036.

Fuck

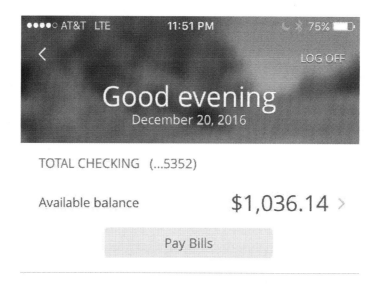

I screenshotted this image of my bank account because I knew I would tell this story some day.

***

The sunlight blinded me as we emerged from the matinee. Families shuffled in and out through the revolving doors, making their happy memories. I was in a daze. Leila led me to the car, her hand wrapped firmly around mine.

"What's wrong? What happened?" she asked.

"The money isn't coming."

"What do you mean?" she asked. "It's delayed?"

I exhaled in defeat. "They are keeping it all."

"Can they do that!?"

"Apparently," I said stoically, trying to maintain my composure in front of her parents.

"What are you gonna do about the commissions?"

"I already paid him. Everything." I said it without looking at her.

Leila's concern turned to dread.

We sat in silence the whole way home. I stared out the window. She held my hand in hers. It was more comforting than I anticipated. *We'll get through this.*

30 days earlier . . .

I had decided to go all in on this new business I called "Gym Launch." Here was the idea: I would fly around the country to gyms and fill them up to full capacity using this new methodology that hinged on an offer I had perfected when I owned my chain of gyms.

Leading up to this moment, I had sold five of my six gyms. The funds from selling them, my life's work, I had put into an account I had with a new partner. This money was supposed to be the seed money for our new company.

I was finally going to realize some level of success.

My alarm went off. I groggily swung my arm over blindly clawing at the bedside table. I switched off the alarm, while Leila managed to sleep through the commotion.

I laid there silently, pulling up the bank accounts — a daily ritual. The balance said $300. Wait. That couldn't be right. There was $46,000 in here yesterday.

My adrenaline surged. Looking closer I saw "*-$45,700 Payment Successful.*"

I was frantic.

The money from selling all of my gyms was gone. I checked where the money went. To my "partner." He had taken all the money out.

Fuck.

The last four years of my life had vanished that fast. I officially had nothing, and even less to show for it. No gyms. No equipment. No employees. Nothing.

I felt dead inside.

Adding insult to injury, in that same 30-day period, my mother was in critical condition because of a near fatal accident (and was still under 24-hour supervision), and I had totalled my car in a head on collision at 60 miles per hour and earned a DUI as my consolation prize.

This was the cherry on top. My one saving grace during this time was selling a new "challenge offer" at a gym and collecting all the cash up front as my "fee" for turning their business around.

So I did the only thing I knew. I *sold*. My salesman had done $120,000 in a single month, and I owed him a $22,000 commission check.

The problem was the $120,000 never came.

"We need to talk," I said as Leila and I went into the other room. I worked up the courage to speak but stared at the floor, embarrassed.

"I've got nothing," I said to her. "I'm a sinking ship, and you don't have to stay with me."

She grabbed my chin and pulled my face towards hers so she could look into my eyes: "I would sleep with you under a bridge if it came to that." I would have cried tears of joy, but I was so emotionally exhausted my response appeared apathetic.

I wouldn't stay with me.

"Are we still gonna do these launches starting tomorrow?" She asked. "All my friends quit their jobs to do this." She was being matter of fact, but it still stung. I felt defeated. "Listen, this could go horribly wrong, "

"I trust you. We'll figure it out."

I had two things left at that point: a grand slam offer and an old business credit card with a $100,000 limit from when I had my gyms.

On the day after Christmas (two days after the gut-wrenching call with the payment processor) we were scheduled to launch six new gyms . . . at the same time. Between airfare, hotels, rental cars, gas, and ad spend (all multiplied by six), I was going to be spending $3,300 per *day* of money I didn't have. My last dollar had gone to paying my salesman. I still remember my hand shaking as the advertisements went live: Off→ ON.

Just like that, I was going into debt at a rate of $412 dollars per working hour. Just like that, $3,300 per day began getting deducted from my account.

-$3,300 . . . I now officially have nothing

-$3,300 . . . I now have officially less than nothing

-$3,300 . . . I have $10,000 less than nothing

-$3,300 . . . This one decision is going to ruin my future forever.

But things started shaping up. Here's what happened that month (January 2017), as documented by my old processing records I dug up. You can see the month along the left column and the revenue collected that month along the right.

	Pending Authorizations		Charges		Refunds		Rtns/Chgbks		Voids		Declines		Totals	
	Count	Amount	Count	Amount	Count	Amount	Count	Amount	Count	Amount	Count	Aprvl Pct	Count	Amount
01/2017	0	$0.00	348	$102,605.64	7	$-2,488.33	0	$0.00	12	$2,002.98	148	70%	515	$100,117.31
02/2017	0	$0.00	847	$190,809.50	56	$-13,243.77	1	$-166.00	5	$1,247.00	232	78%	1141	$177,399.73
03/2017	0	$0.00	782	$177,820.58	61	$-12,701.50	4	$-997.00	21	$3,458.50	285	73%	1153	$164,122.08
04/2017	0	$0.00	704	$204,461.25	49	$-10,725.00	10	$-6,315.00	2	$-50.00	354	67%	1119	$187,421.25
05/2017	0	$0.00	191	$260,754.00	4	$-797.00	11	$-16,984.00	0	$0.00	42	82%	248	$242,973.00
06/2017	0	$0.00	214	$272,835.00	5	$-1,498.00	30	$-55,375.00	0	$0.00	1	100%	250	$215,962.00
07/2017	0	$0.00	282	$316,917.98	0	$0.00	21	$-23,450.00	0	$0.00	7	98%	310	$293,467.98
08/2017	0	$0.00	346	$393,370.62	0	$0.00	28	$-32,998.99	1	$100.00	45	88%	420	$360,371.63
09/2017	0	$0.00	478	$543,376.29	1	$-1,000.00	64	$-65,792.00	0	$0.00	41	92%	584	$476,584.29
10/2017	0	$0.00	799	$828,709.31	7	$-5,798.00	50	$-49,887.00	8	$8,000.00	31	96%	895	$773,024.31
11/2017	0	$0.00	1076	$1,132,319.31	8	$-8,000.00	66	$-64,296.00	1	$1.00	92	92%	1243	$1,060,023.31
12/2017	0	$0.00	1315	$1,363,956.31	13	$-17,296.00	83	$-82,099.00	1	$1,000.00	111	92%	1523	$1,264,561.31
01/2018	0	$0.00	1609	$1,621,972.81	15	$-28,175.00	97	$-88,995.00	8	$9,000.00	102	94%	1831	$1,504,802.81
Totals	0	$0.00	8991	$7,409,908.60	226	$-101,722.60	465	$-487,354.99	59	$24,759.48	1491	86%	11232	$6,820,831.01

We made $100,117! It was just enough to cover the $3,300/day that had been coming off the credit card. It was actually working. I could hardly believe it. I threw the hail mary, and the universe caught it. I went from looking up bankruptcy lawyers to figuring out what to do with $3,000,000 in profits, accrued within the first twelve months. It felt surreal. And in hindsight, it still kind of does.

By the end of the year we were doing $1,500,000+/mo. Twelve months from then, $4,400,000/mo. Per. Month. Twenty-four months after that, we crossed $120,000,000 in sales, donated $2,000,000 to help fund equal opportunity in low income areas. We met and befriended Arnold Swarzenegger (lifelong hero) and were asked to be board members of his charity *After School All Stars*.

Leila and I meeting with Arnold Schwarzengger at his home. We are now on the national board of his charity After School All Stars. Creating Grand Slam Offers has given us access to people we only dreamed of.

Twelve months after that, we now have a portfolio of seven eight-figure, and multi-eight-figure companies across a variety of industries (photography, publishing, fitness, business consulting, beauty) and business types (brick & mortar chains, software, service, e-commerce, training & education). Our portfolio companies now do about $1,600,000 *per week* (and growing).

I say this because I honestly can't believe it. All of this was because of a girl who believed in me, a credit card, and a Grand Slam Offer.

I know I teleported you from rags to riches. And the natural question is *how?* That's what I'm going to use the rest of this book (and remaining books & free courses in this Acquisition.com series) to break down.

The skill of making offers saved me from bankruptcy and likely saved my life. I have made so many mistakes in my life. I've made so many bad life decisions. I've hurt people knowingly and mistakenly. I've done bad things with good intentions. I say this because I am human. I don't pretend to have the answers. I have my own demons that I battle everyday. But, despite my many shortcomings, I've still managed to get really good at this *one* thing . . . and I'd like to share it with you. I can teach you how to build great offers.

I don't know who you are (yes, you, the one reading this). But thank you from the bottom of my heart. Thank you for allowing me to do work I find meaningful. Thank you for giving me your most valuable asset — your attention. I promise to do my best to give you a positive return on it.

Here is your first piece of good news: if you are reading this, then you are already in the top 10 percent. Most people buy stuff and then promptly ignore it. I can also throw out a spoiler: the further you get in the book, the bigger the nuggets become. Just watch.

This book delivers.

The world needs more entrepreneurs. It needs more fighters. It needs more magic. And that's what I'm sharing with you — magic.

Grand Slam Offers

"Make people an offer so good they would feel stupid saying no."

- Travis Jones

I was 23 years old and, to quote Ruth from Ozark, I didn't know "shit about fuck." But there I was, in a Las Vegas penthouse hotel room along with ten business owners learning about marketing and sales… in my most-fashionable "beast mode" t-shirt (a shirt I had gotten for free, and one of the five shirts I owned at the time).

Truthfully, I was anxious, self-conscious, and thought I was making a huge mistake. I had paid $3,000 of money I didn't have to get a seat at the table. I knew I needed to learn. Everyone there had a business . . . except me. I was planning on starting one, a gym.

TJ, the organizer, had multiple successful businesses. While going over the agenda, I remember he made an off-hand comment about making $1,000,000 that year.

One. Million. Dollars. I was spellbound. *I wanna be like this guy. I'll do anything.* The problem was, I didn't know what any of them were talking about. KPIs? CPLs? Conversion rates? My head was spinning as I pretended like I knew what they were talking about. But I didn't, and I'm bad at pretending.

Between "sessions," TJ found me. He could tell I was in way over my head. TJ was kind, curious, and caring. After a little bit of small talk, he asked me a simple question that changed my life forever . . .

"Do you want to know the secret to sales?"

I had never sold anything in my life. I had never even read a book on it. I had just recently learned what the term meant (seriously). I leaned forward, intent to download every syllable he spoke right into my brain.

I opened my notepad and stared at him with intent. I was ready for *the* secret.

He looked at me soberly and said: "Make people an offer so good they would feel stupid saying no."

I nodded, wrote it down, underlined it, and circled it. And with that, my entire worldview of selling was transformed.

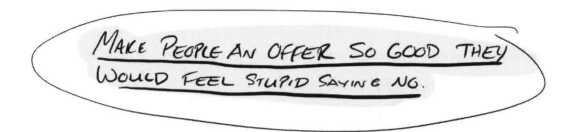

MAKE PEOPLE AN OFFER SO GOOD THEY WOULD FEEL STUPID SAYING NO.

My mind began racing. I didn't have to be skilled . . . or even any good. I just had to come up with things that *anyone* would say yes to. The greatest game of my life had begun.

What This Book Is About

At some point, every successful business owner was a *wantrepreneur*. A person full of ideas and frustrated at having potential to spare. Something clicks when they realize the horrible trade they (and so many people) make — trading their freedom for (falsely) perceived security.

Their discomfort compounds. And once the discomfort of staying the same surpasses the discomfort of change, they take the leap. *I'm going to be an entrepreneur so I can be free. Free to do whatever I want, whenever I want, with whomever I want.*

Some learned about entrepreneurship through personal development.

Others got into it through a franchise.

Others bought courses.

And some just said, "F*CK IT. I'm doing it. I'll make it work."

And made it work they did.

Most of us open up shop with the intention of helping people in some way. Many times, this assistance is in some way related to something that's affected us personally. We set out to "give back" by providing value to others by helping them solve a problem that once plagued us. Then again, sometimes this isn't our way in. In either case, we cling to the dream of making more and being freer than we are now.

Many of us thought, naively, that owning a business would be our crowning accomplishment — a final destination — when in reality, it was just the beginning.

Somehow, in the transition between "passionate to help others" and "owning my first business," we gradually realized that we don't even know the first thing about business, let alone turning a profit.

We may know a lot about our passion, about *why* we started the business, but that doesn't mean we know anything about succeeding in business. Much to the disappointment of the idealists on the sidelines, succeeding in business means getting prospective customers to trade us money for our services. Our passion for their hard-earned coins. That's the agreement. The only way to facilitate that exchange, to transact, to literally carry out business as a business *is by making the prospect an offer.*

What's An Offer Anyways?

The *only* way to conduct business is through a value exchange, a trade of dollars for value. The offer is what initiates this trade. In a nutshell, the offer is the goods and services you agree to give or provide, how you accept payment, and the terms of the agreement. It is what *begins* the process of getting customers and making money. It is the first thing any new customer will interact with in your business. Since the offer is what attracts new customers, it is the lifeblood of your business.

No offer? No business. No life.

Bad offer? Negative profit. No business. Miserable life.

Decent offer? No profit. Stagnating business. Stagnating life.

Good offer? Some profit. Okay business. Okay life.

Grand Slam Offer? Fantastic profit. Insane business. Freedom.

This book helps entrepreneurs craft those Grand Slam Offers. These are the offers that are so effective, profitable, and life-changing that it seems they can only be the result of luck! That's how it looks to an untrained eye, at least.

As you likely now know, I have crafted thousands of offers over the last decade. Most failed. Some did okay. And some struck gold . . . but I never *really* knew why. As Dr Burgelman, a famous Stanford business school professor said, it is far better to have understood why you failed than to be ignorant of why you succeeded.

But, as the data started rolling in, what seemed like "luck" and "fortune" was closer to a repeatable framework. I have been fortunate enough to have struck gold enough times to document these frameworks and have gotten "lightning to strike twice."

I have put the steps and components of those frameworks in a logical and digestible format so they are actually useful. Today. Like now. I'm giving you action. Instead of a sad-but-typical book of vague business theories and mental masturbation.

The Two Main Problems Most Entrepreneurs Face and How This Book Solves Them

Although you *can* make the list of problems you face a mile long, which is a great way to stress yourself out, all these problems typically stem from two big kahunas:

1) Not enough clients

2) Not enough cash (excess profit at the end of the month)

Seems obvious, right? It costs more money and time to get more clients, thereby solving issue one, and that money is coming from the profit margins, which creates problem two! What's more annoying, prospects savagely compare and belittle our services in favor of cheaper and crappier alternatives — with the cheapest one "winning." This, of course, when "winning" means getting to work more for even less (sad face).
Let's say you've slashed prices to get more customers. You may even have a full client load. But here you are, barely making it because profit margins are too thin. "Competition" becomes a race to the bottom.

If you're struggling with one or both of these issues, you're not alone. I've been there. Heck, I think *every* entrepreneur has these same challenges.

I also want you to know that it's not your fault. Typical models weren't designed for profit maximization. They were designed by companies who have boatloads of funding and can operate at a loss for *years*. When these models are used in the real world, business owners just barely "get by." They essentially "buy themselves a job" and work 100 hours a week to avoid working 40. Crappy trade. My guess is that if you're anything like me, you signed up for something better.

Keep an open-mind. The contents of this book, if executed, can transform your business . . . fast.

It's okay if you're not into money numbers or business models. I've done all that work for you. I'm walking you through the process step-by-step in these pages. I'm going to explain each of the big two problems we touched on above in detail, including why they don't work. Then I'm going to show you the solutions. And to wrap this adventure up, I'll explain how to enhance value to maximize how much you make per customer, so that you can outmarket everyone and stack cash.

We use this offer model for every niche we work with (chiros, dentists, gyms, agencies, plumbers, roofers, dog walkers, physical products, software, brick and mortar stores, and so many more), and it's amazing how fast things can improve with each and every one of them when they use this framework.

What's In It For You?

I've made every (dumb) business mistake in the book. Now, you can learn from my embarrassing, brutal, multi-million dollar fuck-ups without having to suffer the pain yourself.

Building these businesses has been a very hard and emotional journey for me. I wouldn't trade these experiences for the world. However, if this book helps just one entrepreneur avoid suffering as I did, keep their business open, or accomplish their dreams, it will all be worth it.

If you are willing to exchange the time it takes to watch two episodes of your favorite tv show and really study this book — and if you *implement* even a single offer component — I can guarantee you will add more clients and more dollars to your bottom line. Reading this book, and taking it to heart, will be the single best return on time for your business. Nothing else will allow you to do what this book can do in the same amount of time. That is a promise.

As a side benefit — implementing a new offer is about one of the easiest things to do in a business. So you really *can* do this. This isn't some management practice or culture building hoodoo. This is the real "how you sell shit for lots of money"-type stuff.

What's In It For Me?

I give all these materials (this book, the accompanying course, and all other books and courses which you can find at *acquisition.com*) for free or at cost in order to help as many people as humanly possible make more and serve more. And I have made these with the intention of providing more value than you can get from a $1000 course, any $30,000 coaching program, and hilariously more than a $200,000 college degree. And I do this because, although I could sell these materials in that format, *I just don't want to*. I've made my money *doing* this stuff, not *teaching how to do* this stuff, contrary to most of the marketing community at large. So my model is different (I'll explain more in a second).

That being said, there are two key archetypes I am looking to provide value to with my published materials. For archetype I, entrepreneurs *under* $3,000,000 per year in revenue, my goal is to help you get there and *earn your trust.* Try just a couple of tactics from this book, watch them work, then try a few more, watch them work . . . and so on. The more you see results in your own business, the better.

Once you succeed, you become archetype II, entrepreneurs *at minimum between* $3M - $10M in yearly revenue. Once you get there, or if that's you now, I'd be honored to invest in your business and help you cross $30M, $50M, or $100M+. I don't sell coaching, masterminds, courses, or anything like that. Instead, I have a portfolio of companies I take an equity interest in. I use the infrastructure, resources, and teams of all my companies to fast track their growth.

But don't believe me yet...*we just met.*

If you're curious, my business model is simple, just like the four-piece pyramid logo:

---

(1) Provide value at no cost far in excess of what the rest of the marketplace charges for.

(2) Have entrepreneurs use materials that actually work and make money helping more folks

(3) Earn the trust of the hyper-executor business owners who use the frameworks to scale their businesses to $3M-$10M per year and beyond

(4) Invest in those businesses to make more impact at scale while helping everyone else for free.

If you look carefully, the process reverse-engineers success. I think it's pretty cool. Here's how: I know these business owners can execute the frameworks I have without hand-holding, and therefore, would be very likely to succeed with the next set of frameworks (getting to $30M, $50M, $100M looks different than getting to $3-$10M). They know that my style works for them, because it already has. So we operate on shared trust - I trust they can execute, and they trust that our stuff works - again, because it already has….all while helping everyone else….fo' free. So it allows me to preemptively avoid failures and dramatically increases success likelihood. Let me show you how much….

At the time of this writing, every business I have started since March of 2017 has achieved a $1,500,000/mo run rate. According to the Small Business Administration, the odds of a single business even achieving $10M/year in revenue are .4%, or 1 in 250. Having it happen four times in a row is .4% x .4% x .4% x .4%= very very low probability that it was luck. As such, I can say with conviction that we know how to recreate success using the frameworks I share over and over again. They work because they are timeless business principles.

I actively visualize, every day, how it felt to wake up in the middle of the night in cold sweats, wondering how I'd make payroll. That gut-wrenching "meditation" keeps me hungry as an entrepreneur but also grateful for my security and peace of mind. I want the latter for you and anyone else that gives a damn about what they do.

Fair enough?

Cool. So let's get to it.

Basic Outline of This Book

This book is intended to be a resource. As a resource, I mean it will be something you will read through and then keep in your tool box, coming back to it again and again. Why? As Einstein says, "never memorize anything you can look up." Business is not a spectator sport. You're not cramming for some midterm, and you're not some limp-wristed philosopher.

You do work. And to work, you need tools. This, my friend, is one of those tools.

<u>General Outline</u>

- Section I: How We Got Here (You Just Finished It)

- Section II: Pricing: How To Charge Lots of Money For Stuff

- Section III: Value: Create Your Offer: How To Make Something So Good People Line Up To Buy

- Section IV: Enhancing Your Offer: How To Make Your Offer So Good They Feel Stupid Saying No

- Section V: Next Steps: How To Make This Happen In The Real World

> **For free courses and books so good they grow your business without your consent, go to: <u>Acquisition.com</u>.**

SECTION II
Pricing

How To Charge Lots of Money For Stuff

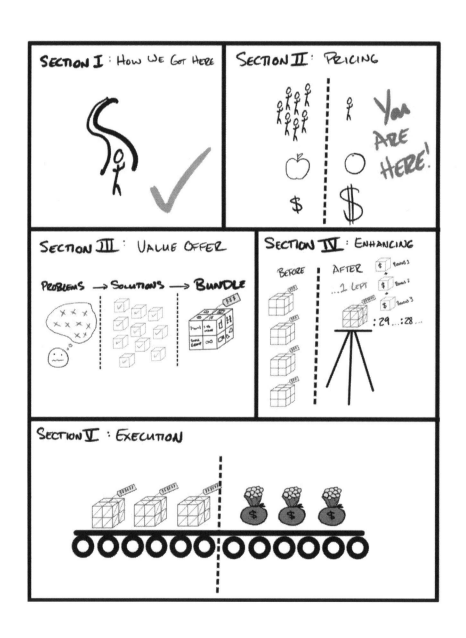

Pricing: The Commodity Problem

"Think different."

- Steve Jobs

"Grow or Die" is a core tenet at our companies. We believe every person, every company, and every organism is either growing or dying. Maintenance is a myth.

What this means is, if your company isn't growing, it's dying. This is a sobering reality for many of us. I learned the hard way, and my businesses suffered for a long time because of it.

Let me explain. The market is continuously growing. The stock market grows at 9 percent per year. If we aren't growing at 9 percent per year, we are falling behind. "Maintenance," in the most generic sense, would be 9 percent growth year over year.

Furthermore, if you're in a growing marketplace, then you might have to grow at 20-30 percent per year, just to keep up, or risk falling behind. So you can see how maintenance is a myth.

So, then,what does it take to grow? Thankfully, just three simple things:

1) Get more customers

2) Increase their average purchase value

3) Get them to buy more times

That's it.

Sure, there are lots of ways to acquire customers and zillions of ways to increase order value and purchase frequency, but, simply put, that's it. Those are the only three ways to grow.

Example: If I sell 10 clients a month, and a client is worth $1,000 to me over their lifetime (through avg cart value x avg number of purchases), then my business will cap at $10,000/mo (10 x $1,000).

10 New Clients/mo x $1000 Lifetime Value = $10,000/mo max revenue.

If you want to grow, you've got to either sell more clients every month (while maintaining suitable margins) or have them be worth more (by increasing the profit per purchase or number of times they buy). That's it.

Author Note - Only Two Ways to Grow

To simplify this concept even more. There are really only two ways to grow: get more customers, and increase each customer's value. "Increasing each customer's value" has two sub-buckets: 1) Increasing profit per purchase 2) Increasing the number of times they buy. For the purpose of this book, I highlight both of those sub-buckets as individual growth paths. I did this because I think it will be easier to understand the money models that will come in Volume III. All three — getting more customers, increasing their average purchase value, and getting them to buy more — are repeated themes in this book. But if you seek simplicity, both increasing average purchase value and increasing the number of times a customer buys results in one outcome: increasing each customer's value.

Business Terms

Before going any further, and to better flesh out the concepts that follow, we should take a second to define and better understand some key business concepts. When I stood in that Las Vegas penthouse in my "beast mode" t-shirt I was clueless about such terms. Let me help you be better than, well, me.

Gross Profit: The revenue minus the direct cost of servicing an ADDITIONAL customer. If I sell lotion for $10 and it costs me $2, my gross profit is $8 or 80 percent. If I sell agency services for $1,000/mo and it costs me $100/mo in labor to run that client's advertising, then my gross profit is $900 or 90 percent. Note: This is *not* net profit. Net profit is what's left over after *all* expenses are paid, not just the direct costs of fulfillment.

Lifetime Value: The gross profit accrued over the entire lifetime of a customer. This is gross profit multiplied by the number of purchases an average customer will make over their lifetime. Using the example above, if the average customer stays five months, and they pay $1,000/mo while it costs me $100 per month to fulfill, then their lifetime value is $4,500.

Here's the breakdown:

Revenue: ($1,000/mo * 90% Gross Margin * 5 months) = $4,500 Lifetime Value (LTV)

Note that the indirect costs, like admin, software, rent, etc., are not included in LTV.

Note: You will find different definitions for lifetime value depending on the source. The biggest difference is that some sources only count total revenue, while others focus on gross profit over the lifespan. I focus on gross profit. You may also see me refer to this as **LTGP Lifetime Gross Profit** in other texts for clarity's sake.

Value-Driven vs. Price-Driven Purchases

This book was intended to be a textbook for any business that wants to *grow*. I've spent (and continue to spend) hundreds of hours on calls and in-person meetings consulting entrepreneurs on crafting their offers. I have seen the ones that take off into the stratosphere and those that fizzle.

Having a Grand Slam offer makes it almost impossible to lose. But why? What gives it such an impact? In short, having a Grand Slam Offer helps with all *three* of the requirements for growth: getting more customers, getting them to pay more, and getting them to do so more times.

How? It allows you to differentiate yourself from the marketplace. In other words, it allows you to sell your product based on VALUE not on PRICE.

Commoditized = Price Driven Purchases (race to the bottom)

Differentiated = Value Driven Purchases (sell in a category of one with no comparison. Yes, market matters, which I will expound on in the next chapter)

A commodity, as I define it, is a product available from many places. For that reason, it's prone to purchases based on "price" instead of "value." If all products are "equal," then the cheapest one is the most valuable by default. In other words, if a prospect compares your product to another and thinks "these are pretty much the same, I'll buy the cheaper one," then they commoditized you. How embarrassing! But really . . . it's one of the worst experiences a value-driven entrepreneur can have.

This is a massive problem for the entrepreneur because commodities are valued at the point of market efficiency. This means that the marketplace drives the price down through competition until the margins are *just* enough to keep the lights on: "just enough" to become a slave to their business. The business makes "just enough" to justify the owner waiting anxiously for things to "turn around," and by the time that lie is realized . . . they are in too deep to pivot (at least, until now).

A Grand Slam Offer solves this problem.

But What Does A Grand Slam Offer Do?

Alright, let's start by defining a Grand Slam Offer.

It's an offer you present to the marketplace that cannot be compared to any other product or service available, combining an attractive promotion, an unmatchable value proposition, a premium price, and an unbeatable guarantee with a money model (payment terms) that allows you to *get paid* to get new customers . . . forever removing the cash constraint on business growth.

In other words, it allows you to sell in a "category of one," or, to apply another great phrase, to "sell in a vacuum." The resulting purchasing decision for the prospect is now between your product *and nothing*. So you can sell at whatever price you get the prospect to perceive, not in comparison to anything else. As a result, it gets you more customers, at higher ticket prices, for less money. If you like fancy marketing terms, it breaks down like this:

1) Increased Response Rates (think clicks)

2) Increased Conversion (think sales)

3) Premium Prices (think charging a lot of money).

Having a Grand Slam Offer increases your response rates to advertisements (aka more people will click or take an action on an advertisement they see containing a Grand Slam Offer).

If you pay the same amount for eyeballs but 1) more people respond, 2) more of those responses buy, and 3) they buy for higher prices, your business *grows*.

I've "struck gold" on my share of offers. Not because I've got some superpower, but because I've just done this a lot of times (and failed even more). I sorted through the crap that chronically fails and pocketed all the stuff that reproducibly succeeds (and put it in this book) .

Here's the key takeaway from all this: a business does the *same* work in both cases (with a commoditized or a Grand Slam Offer). The fulfillment is the same. But if one business uses a Grand Slam Offer and another uses a "commodity" offer, the Grand Slam Offer makes that business appear as if it has a totally different product — and that means a value-driven, versus price-driven, purchase.

If you have a "commodity" offer, you will compete on price (having a price-driven purchase versus a value-driven purchase). Your Grand Slam Offer, however, forces a prospect to stop and *think differently* to assess the value of your differentiated product. Doing this establishes you as your own category, which means it's too difficult to compare prices, which means *you* re-calibrate the prospect's value-meter.

Real Life Grand Slam Offer Money Math: Before and After

Quick backstory . . . one of our companies is a software that advertising agencies use to work leads for their customers. Using this software, agencies transform their offer from a commoditized offer of lead generation services to a Grand Slam Offer of "pay for performance." Let me show you the multiplicative effect it has on the revenue of the business.

While rounded for illustration's sake, these values are based on the real numbers a lead generation agency selling services to brick and mortar businesses experience

27

Old Commoditized Way (Price-Driven) — Race to the bottom

Commoditized Offer: $1,000 down, then $1,000/mo retainer for agency services

Metric	Commodity	Grand Slam	Explanation
Advertising Spend	$10,000		Dollars Spent on advertising
Impressions Reached	300,000		Eyeballs reached from advertising
Response Rate	0.00013		Percentage of people who book call (CTR x Optin %)
Appts Booked	40		# of Appointments Booked as a result
Show Rate	75%		Percentage of people who book call
Appts Showed	30		# of people who show up for their appt
Closing %	16%		% of people who purchase
Appts Closed	5		# of people who purchase
Price	$1,000		The amount that people put down to begin service
Total	$5,000		Total amount of up front cash collected
ROAS	.5 : 1		Return on Advertising Spend (ROAS)

Breakdown: At .5 to 1 return on advertising spend, you lose money getting customers. But in 30 days, those 5 customers will pay another $1,000 each, bringing you to $10,000 in total and break even. The next month, the $5,000 that comes in would be your first profitable month, and each month thereafter would be profitable (assuming they all stay).

This is an example of a commoditized service — normal agency work. There's a million of them, and they all look the same. Commoditized businesses and offers have a harder time getting responses from ads because all their marketing looks the same as everyone else's.

> **Note:** It all looks the same because they are all making the same offer.
>
> *You pay us to work.*
>
> *We do work.*
>
> *Maybe you get results from that work. Maybe you don't.*

It's reasonable, but it's easily duplicated (and subject to commoditization). *This commoditization creates a price-driven purchase . . .*

You are forced to be priced "competitively" to get clients *and* to stay that way to keep them. If the client sees a cheaper version of the "same thing," then the value discrepancy will cause them to swap providers. This is a dilemma . . . lose this client, the rest of your clients, and potential clients, or stay "competitive." Your margins become so thin they *vanish*.

Furthermore, it's hard to get prospects to say yes (and *keep* them saying yes) unless you're hypervigilant about clients commoditizing your business by staying "competitive." And that's the problem with the old commoditized way. They're able to compare. Unless you switch to a Grand Slam Offer, your prices will keep getting beaten down. The business eventually dies, or the entrepreneur throws in the towel. No bueno.

We want to make an offer that's so different that you can skip the awkward explanation of why your product is different from everyone elses (which, if they have to ask, then they are probably too ignorant to understand the explanation) and instead just have the offer do that work for you. That's the Grand Slam Offer way.

Let's dive in to see the contrast in sales numbers.

New Grand Slam Offer Way (Differentiated, Incomparable) (Value-Driven)

Grand Slam Offer: Pay one time. (No recurring fee. No retainer.) Just cover ad spend. I'll generate leads and work your leads for you. And only pay me if people show up. And I'll guarantee you get 20 people in your first month, or you get your next month free. I'll also provide all the best practices from the other businesses like yours.

- Daily sales coaching for your staff

- Tested scripts

- Tested price points and offers to swipe and deploy

- Sales recordings

. . . and everything else you need to sell and fulfill your customers. I'll give you the entire play book for (insert industry), absolutely free just for becoming a client.

In a nutshell, I'm feeding people into your business, showing you, exactly, how to sell them so that you can get the highest prices, which means that you make the most money possible . . . sound fair enough?

It's clear these are drastically different offers . . . but so what? Where's the *money*!? Let's compare both in the below chart.

Metric	Commodity	Grand Slam	Difference
Advertising Spend	$10,000	$10,000	Unchanged
Impressions Reached	300,000	300,000	Unchanged
Response Rate	0.00013	0.00033	**2.5x Response (more appealing, so more respond)**
Appts Booked	40	100	Result
Show Rate	75%	75%	Unchanged
Appts Showed	30	75	Result
Closing %	16%	37%	**2.3x Closing (more value, so more buy)**
Appts Closed	5	28	Result
Price	$1,000	$3,997	**4x Price (one time fee vs recurring)**
Total	$5,000	$112,000	**22.4x Cash Up Front Collected**
ROAS	.5 : 1	11.2 : 1	**Get paid to get customers.**

Breakdown: You spend the same amount of money for the same eyeballs. Then, you get 2.5x more people to respond to your advertisement because it's a more compelling offer. From there, you close 2.5x as many people because the offer is so much more compelling. From there, you are able to charge a 4x higher price up front. The end result is 2.5 x 2.5 x 4 = 22.4x more cash collected up front. Yes, you spent $10,000 to make $112,000. You just *made money* getting new customers.

Comparison: Remember the old way, the way you lost half the ad spend up front? With the new way, you are making *more* money *and* getting *more* customers. This means that your cost to acquire a customer is so cheap (relative to how much you make) that your limiting factor becomes your ability to do the work you already love doing. Cash flow and acquiring customers is no longer your bottleneck because it's 22.4x more profitable than the old model. Yup. You read that right. This is the part in the action movie where you walk away from an explosion in slow motion.

This is the exact Grand Slam Offer we used with our software business that serves agencies. The numbers can become wild . . . fast. I know 22.4x better sounds unreasonable, but that's the point. If you play the same game everyone else does, you'll get the same results everyone else does (mediocre). You hit singles and doubles, keep the lights on, but never get ahead. But remember the opening passage of this book: that when you align all the pieces, you can knock it out of the park so well that you win *for good*. In my first 18 months in business, we went from $500k/year to $28,000,000/yr off of less than $1M in ad spend. So, when I say 20:1 . . . 50:1 . . . 100:1 returns, I mean it. When you get this right, the results are, well . . . unbelievable.

Summary Points

This chapter illustrated the basic problem with commoditization and how Grand Slam Offers solve that. This gets you out of the pricing war and into a category of one. The next chapter will focus on finding the correct market to apply our pricing strategies to. It's one of the most important things to get right. A grand slam offer given to the wrong audience will fall on deaf ears. We want to avoid that at all costs. We must detour from pricing for a moment to learn what to look for in a market. It's an essential box to check before continuing on our journey.

> **FREE GIFT #1 BONUS TUTORIAL: "START HERE"**
>
> If you want a deeper dive, go to Acquisition.com/training/offers and watch the first video in the free course (starring yours truly) about how I differentiate offers in businesses I consult with and get them to charging premium prices. I also created some Free SOPs/Cheat Codes for you to use so you can implement faster. It's absolutely free. Enjoy.

Pricing: Finding The Right Market -- A Starving Crowd

The seed that fell on good soil represents those who truly hear and understand God's word and produce a harvest of thirty, sixty, or even a hundred times as much as had been planted!"

- Matthew 13:23 (NLT)

A marketing professor asked his students, "If you were going to open a hotdog stand, and you could only have *one* advantage over your competitors . . . which would it be . . . ?"

"Location! ….Quality! …. Low prices! ….Best taste!"

The students kept going until eventually they had run out of answers. They looked at each other waiting for the professor to speak. The room finally fell quiet.

The professor smiled and replied, *"A starving crowd."*

You could have the worst hot dogs, terrible prices, and be in a terrible location, but if you're the only hot dog stand in town and the local college football game breaks out, you're going to sell out. That's the value of a starving crowd.

At the end of the day, if there is a ton of demand for a solution, you can be mediocre at business, have a terrible offer, and have no ability to persuade people, and you can *still* make money.

An example of this was the toilet paper shortage at the beginning of Covid-19. There was no offer. The pricing was atrocious. And there was no compelling sales pitch. But because the crowd was so big and so starving, rolls of toilet paper were going for $100 or more. That's the value of a starving crowd.

Selling Newspapers

A good friend of mine, Lloyd, owned a software business that served newspapers for almost a decade. They set up digital ad services on newspaper websites with a few clicks and instantly helped them sell a whole new ad product. He only charged them a percentage of the revenue he added. So if they made nothing, neither did he. It was pure gain for the papers and a great offer.

But, despite having a great offer and natural sales ability, his business began to decline. Being a high-achieving entrepreneur, he tried all the different angles to solve the problem — *but nothing worked*. He couldn't figure out what the issue was. It was hard for me to see him struggle with this because I think Lloyd is much smarter than I am, and the answer seemed obvious to me. But watching him go through this has been a lesson I have taken with me for life. Before I reveal it, what do you think the problem was? Product? Offer? Marketing and sales? His team?

Let's break it down. It wasn't his product — that was great. It wasn't his offer — he had a zero risk revshare model. It wasn't his sales skills — he was a natural salesman. So, then what was the problem? *He was selling to newspapers!* His market was shrinking by 25 percent *every year*! He had looked at all the angles, except for the most obvious one. Finally, after years of fighting an uphill battle in his market, he realized his market was the source of his problems and decided to downsize his company.

Don't worry — this story has a second half. To illustrate the power of a market, as soon as COVID hit, Lloyd pivoted. He started an automated mask manufacturing company. With new technology, he brought the cost per mask below what people could buy them for from China. Within five months he was doing *millions per month*. Same entrepreneur. Different market. He applied his *same* skill set to a business *he had zero experience in* and was able to win. That's the power of picking the right market.

I give you that story as a cautionary tale. *Your market matters.* Lloyd is a *very* smart human. He is obviously very capable. But we can all be blinded as entrepreneurs because we don't like to give up. We are so accustomed to solving impossible problems that we will keep ramming our heads into the wall. We hate quitting. But the reality is that everyone is affected by their market.

So how do you pick the right market?

What To Look For

There is a market in desperate need of your abilities. You need to find it. And when you do, you will capitalize, all while wondering what took you so long. Don't be romantic about your audience. Serve the people who can pay you what you're worth. And remember that picking a market, like anything, is always our choice, so choose wisely.

In order to sell anything, you need demand. We are not trying to *create* demand. We are trying to *channel* it. That is a very important distinction. If you don't have a market for your offer, nothing that follows will work. This entire book sits atop the assumption that you have at least a "normal" market, which I define as a market that is growing at the same rate as the marketplace and that has common unmet needs that fall into one of three categories: improved health, increased wealth, or improved relationships. For example Lloyd, from the above newspaper story, could have gone through this entire book and nothing in here would have worked for him. Why? Because he would be targeting newspapers, a dying market.

That being said, having a great market is an advantage. <u>But you can be in a normal market that's growing at an average rate and still make crazy money</u>. Every market I have been in has been a normal market. You just don't *actually* want to be selling ice to eskimos.

Here are the basic tenets of what I look for in markets. Let's run through them before we return to the offer.

When picking markets, I look for four indicators:

1) Massive Pain

They must not want, but desperately need, what I am offering. Pain can be anything that frustrates people about their lives. Being broke is painful. A bad marriage is painful. Waiting in line at the grocery stores is painful. Back pain . . . ugly smile pain . . . overweight pain . . . Humans suffer a lot. So for us entrepreneurs, endless opportunity abounds.

The degree of the pain will be proportional to the price you will be able to charge (more on this in the Value Equation chapter). When they hear the solution to their pain, and inversely, what their life would look like *without* this pain, they should be drawn to your solution.

I have a saying I use to train sales teams *"The pain is the pitch."* If you can articulate the pain a prospect is feeling accurately, they will almost always buy what you are offering. A prospect must have a painful problem for us to solve and charge money for our solution.

Pro Tip

The point of good writing is for the reader to *understand*.

The point of good persuasion is for the prospect to feel *understood*.

---

2) Purchasing Power

A friend of mine had a very good system for helping people improve their resumes to get more job interviews. He was great at it. But try as he did, he just could not get people to pay for his services. Why? Because they were all unemployed!

This, again, may seem obvious. But he thought, *"These people are easy to target. They're in massive pain. There are plenty of them, and it's constantly adding new people. This is a great market!"*

He just forgot a crucial point: your audience needs to be able to afford the service you're charging them for. Make sure your targets have the money, or access to the amount of money, needed to buy your services at the prices you require to make it worth your time.

3) Easy to Target

Let's say you have a perfect market, but no way of finding the people who comprise it. Well, making a Grand Slam Offer will be difficult. I make my life easier by looking for easy-to-target markets. Examples of this are avatars that have associations they belong to, mailing lists, social media groups, channels they all watch, etc. If our potential customers are all gathered together somewhere, then we can market to them. If searching them out, however, is like finding needles in a haystack, then it can be very difficult to get your offer in front of any potentially interested eyes.

This point is tactical. It is reality, not theoretical. For instance, you may *want* to serve rich doctors. But if your ads are being displayed to nursing students, your offer will fall on deaf ears, no matter how good it is. Main point: you want to make sure you can target your ideal audience easily. *(Clarifying point - there is no issue wanting to serve rich doctors, they are easy to find. This is just illustrative that your promotions must be served to the right audience).*

4) Growing

Growing markets are like a tailwind. They make everything move forward faster. Declining markers are like headwinds. They make all efforts harder. This was Lloyd's example. Newspapers had three of the four makings of a great market: (1) lots of pain, (2) purchasing power, (3) easy to target. But they were shrinking (fast). No matter how hard he tried, the entire marketplace was fighting against him. Business is hard enough, and markets move quickly. So you might as well find a good market to give you a tailwind to make the process easier.

Making This Real

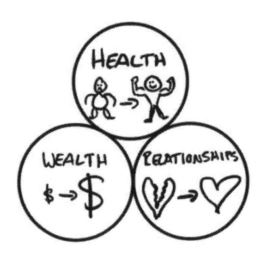

There are three main markets that will always exist: Health, Wealth, and Relationships. The reason that those will always exist is that there is always tremendous pain when you lack them. There is always demand for solutions to these core human pains. The goal is to find a smaller subgroup within one of those larger buckets that is growing, has the buying power, and is easy to target (the other three variables).

So if I were a relationship expert trying to find my avatar, I'd rather focus on "second half of life relationship" coaching for old timers than helping college students in relationships. Why? Because senior citizens who are alone are likely suffering more pain as they are nearer their deaths (pain), have more buying power (money), and are easy to find (targeting). Lastly, at the time of this writing, there are more people turning 65 each year than turning 20 (growing).

That is the idea. Think about what you are good at in regards to health, wealth, and relationships. Then think about who might value your service the most (is in the most pain), has the buying power to pay what *you* want (money), and can be found easily (targeting). As long as those three criteria are strong *and* the market isn't shrinking, you'll be in good shape.

But how important to your success is finding a "great market" versus a "normal market" versus a "bad market?" The answer: it actually depends. Let me explain.

Order of Importance: Three Levers on Success

It's unlikely you are going to be in a dying market like the newspaper example. It's also unlikely you're going to be selling toilet paper in COVID (buying frenzy). You'll likely be in a "normal" market. And that's totally okay. There is a fortune to be made within normal markets. My single point here is that you can't be in a "bad" market, or nothing will work. That being said, here's the simplest illustration of the order of importance between markets, offers, and persuasion skills:

Starving Crowd (market) > Offer Strength > Persuasion Skills

Let's say you were to rate these elements on a scale of great, normal, and bad. You could essentially move down the line from left to right in order of importance. A "great" rating on a higher-order piece overpowers anything else lower on the priority scale. A "normal" rating moves the buck to the next part of the equation. A "bad" stops the equation *unless* a "great" from a higher priority component nullifies it. Here are a few examples:

Example #1: Even if you have a bad offer and are bad at persuasion, you're going to make money if you're in a great market. If you're on the corner hocking hot dogs when the bars close up at 2am, with mobs of starving drunk folks, you're gonna sell out your hotdogs.

Example #2 (most of us): If you are in a normal market and have a Grand Slam Offer (great), you can make tons of money even if you're bad at persuasion. This is most people reading this book. That's why I wrote it — to help you maximize your success by learning to really build a Grand Slam Offer.

Example #3: Let's say you're in a normal market and have a normal offer. In order to be massively successful, you would *have* to be *exceptionally* good at persuasion. Then and only then will you succeed, with your persuasive skills serving as the fulcrum of your success. Heck, many empires have been built by exceptional persuaders. It's just the hardest path to follow and requires the most effort and learning. Nailing your offer helps you shortcut this path to success. Otherwise, you will just have a normal business that takes exceptional skill to be successful (nothing wrong with that, but probably not what you signed up for).

Commit to the Niche

I have a saying when coaching entrepreneurs on picking their target market *"Don't make me niche slap you."*

Too often, a newer entrepreneur half-heartedly tries *one* offer in *one* market, doesn't make a million dollars, then mistakenly thinks "this is a bad market." Most times that's not actually the case. They just haven't found a Grand Slam Offer yet to apply to that market.

They think, *I'll switch from helping dentists to helping chiropractors — that's it!* When, in reality, both of those are normal markets and represent billions of dollars in revenue. Either would work, j*ust not both.* You must pick *one.* No one can serve two masters.

I have coined the term "niche slap" to remind entrepreneurs in my communities to commit once they pick. All businesses and, all markets, have unpleasant characteristics. The grass is never greener once you get to the other side. If you keep hopping from niche to niche, hoping that the market will solve your problems, you deserve to be *niche slapped.*

You must stick with whatever you pick long enough to have trial and error. You will fail. In fact, you will fail until you succeed. But you will fail far longer if you keep changing who you market to, because you must start over from the beginning each time. So, pick then commit.

Riches Are In The Niches

The other reason to commit to the niche is because of how much more you will make. Simply put, niching down will make you far more money.

Author Note - When To Broaden (Advice For Most People)

For most, if you are under $10M per year, niching down will make you more money. After that, it will depend on how narrow the niche is, or, what is called TAM (total addressable market). A business can really only grow to meet the total addressable market. That being said, for most people, getting to $10M per year is already a top .4% achievement (only 1 in 250 businesses achieve this). So for 99.6 percent of readers below $10M per year, it's almost always easier to serve *fewer* clients *more narrowly*. But if you want to go beyond that, you *may* (depending on the size of your TAM) have to broaden your audience by going up market, down market, or into an adjacent market where your existing services can provide value.

For context, many companies expanded to $30M+ per year serving a single niche: Chiropractors, Gyms, Plumbers, Solar, Roofers, Salon Owners, etc. If you are at $1M or $3M, thinking you have capped and must expand, you are wrong. You just need to be better.

When I truly grasped how much more *profit* I was leaving on the table, it changed my life. It was what took me from doing acquisition for *anyone* to teaching it to a specific avatar. In my instance, I decided on a microgym owner with ~100 members, a signed lease, at least one employee, and wanted to help clients lose weight. That's pretty specific compared to "small business owners" or "anyone who will pay me" which is common. And I was very specific. In that business (Gym Launch) - we turned down - and still do - anyone who is not that avatar. That means no personal trainers, no online coaches, etc.

Could I have helped them? Of course I could have. I mean heck, the majority of our portfolio is comprised of non-gym companies. But in order to maintain product focus, and high converting messaging, knowing *exactly* who the product was for was a game changer. It helped us know *exactly* who we were speaking to at all times. And *exactly* whose problems we were solving.

But simplicity and ease may not be enough to sway you, so let me illustrate why honing in on one niche will make you more money.

Reason: you can literally charge 100x more for the *exact* same product. Dan Kennedy was the first person to illustrate this for me, and I will do my best to pass on the torch to you in these pages.

Niching Product Pricing Example:

Example

Product	Price
Time Management	$19
Time Management For Sales Professionals	$99
Time Management For Outbound B2B Sales	$499
Time Management For Outbound B2B Power Tools & Gardening Sales Reps	$1997

Dan Kennedy taught me this (and it changed my life forever). Let's say you sold a generic course on Time Management. Unless you were some massive time management guru with a compelling or unique story, it would be unlikely it would turn into anything significant. What do you think "yet another" time management course is valued at? $19, $29? Sure. Nothing to write home about. Let's just say $19 for illustration sake.

Now we shall unleash the power of niche pricing in various stages on your product

So let's imagine you make the product more specific, keeping the same principles, and call it "Time Management For Sales Professionals." All of a sudden, this course is for a more specific type of person. We could tie their increase to even one more sale or one more deal and it would be worth more. But there are a lot of sales people. So this might be a $99 product. Neat, but we can do better.

So let's go down another level of niching and call our product…. "Time Management for B2B Outbound Sales Reps." Following the same principles of specificity, now we know our sales people probably have very experienced deals and commissions. A single sale would easily net this salesman $500 (or more), so it would be easy to justify a $499 price tag. This is already a 25x increase in price for almost an identical product. I could stop here, but I'm going to go one step further.

Let's just niche down one last level…. "Time Management for B2B Outbound Power Tools & Gardening Sales Reps." Boom.

Think about it for a second, if you were a power tools outbound sales rep, you would think to yourself "This is made exactly for me" and would *happily* fork over maybe $1000 to $2000 for a time management program that could help you achieve your goal.

The actual pieces of the program may be the same as the generic $19 course, but since they have been applied, and the sales messaging could speak so much to this avatar, they will find it more compelling *and* get more value from it in a real way. This concept applies to anything you decide to do. You want to be 'the guy' who services 'this type of person' or solves 'this type of problem.' And even more niched 'I solve this type of problem for this specific type of person in this unique counter-intuitive way that reverses their deepest fear."

That's why a fitness program for generic weight loss might be priced at only $19 while a fitness program designed and marketed only to shift-nurses might be priced at $1997….(even though the core of the program is likely similar - eat less, move more).

End Result: The market matters. Your niche matters. And if you can sell the same product for 100x the price, should you?

I'll let you decide.

Summary Points

The purpose of this chapter is to reinforce two things. First, don't pick a *bad* market. Normal markets are fine. Great markets are great. Second, once you pick, commit to it until you figure it out.

If you try *one hundred offers, I promise* you will succeed. Most people never try anything. Others fail once, then give up. It takes resilience to succeed. Stop personalizing! It's not about you! If your offer doesn't work, it doesn't mean you suck. It means your offer sucks. Big difference. You only suck if you stop trying. So, try again. You'll never become world class if you stop after a failed attempt.

If you find a crazy good market, ride it, and ride it hard. And if you pair a Grand Slam Offer with a crazy market, you'll likely never need to work again (seriously). So have this skill set — the ability to accurately assess markets by taking into account pain, money, targeting, and growth — in your back pocket so that when lightning strikes, you can make sure it strikes twice.

Having established how to nail a market, let's get back to pricing. The first step to making crazy money is charging premium prices.

FREE GIFT #2 BONUS TUTORIAL: WINNING MARKETS

If you want to know more about how I pick markets, and find niches that are profitable, go to Acquisition.com/training/offers course then watch "Winning Markets" for a short video tutorial. I've also included a Free Checklist to see how your market or niche measures up. It's absolutely free, enjoy.

Pricing: Charge What It's Worth

"Charge as high a price as you can say out loud without cracking a smile."

- Dan Kennedy

A picture of Gym Lords Summit 2019 for our highest level gym owners all sporting my trendy mustache.

January 2019.

All I could see was black. My eyes felt glued shut. I was awake, but the fatigue in my temples felt like a five-pound weight was duct-taped to my skull, dragging my eyelids back down. I had to concentrate forcibly to open them.

The details of the dimly lit room beamed in. I rolled over to the edge of the hotel room bed, feeling each and every muscle in my body as my weight shifted. Hunched on my side,

I could see my clothes scattered on the floor. I was so beat the night before that I didn't even remember taking them off.

I had just finished a five-day gauntlet of keynote after keynote presentation. Two days of presentations for our highest-level clients immediately followed by spending two days planning with our entire company (135+ employees).

I had missed a FaceTime call from my father the day before. I didn't have anything on my agenda for the morning. So I creakily got up, slid into a hoodie and some sweats, and walked into the hotel hallway to call him back. After the initial pleasantries, he immediately dove into why he was calling — parental concern.

"I saw the picture you posted of all your clients . . . " he said, but in an unusually concerned tone. "I thought the event was for all your highest-paying clients? I didn't know it was a big event. It looked like you had a thousand people there!"

Alone in the hallway and struggling to shake the heavy weight of exhaustion still, I tried to gauge where his concern was coming from and what he was getting at. I had explained this all to him already. "It was only for our highest-level clients, that wasn't all our clients," I said. "Just the ones who pay $42,000 a year . . . our Gym Lords, like I told you."

"Every single person in that picture paid you $42,000?" He sounded almost frightened at the idea.

"Yeah, wild right?" My voice was hoarse from days of speaking and thousands of twenty-second conversations.

"Is it legal what you're doing?" he asked. *Wow. That escalated quickly, I thought to myself.* "Do they know they're paying you that much?"

"Yes, it's legal. And of course they know. It's not like magically siphoning money."

"That's a lot of money. I hope what you're giving them is worth it."

I contemplated whether it was worth the effort to dive into this or just ignore it. But knowing this was going to be "a thing," I took a deep breath and began to explain. "If I made you $239,000 extra this year, would you pay me $42,000?" I asked, using "$239,000" because it was the average increase in topline revenue of a gym using our systems for 11 months.

"For sure," he said, "I mean if I knew I was going to make that back. But what would I have to do?"

"About 15 hours a week of work"

"And how long would it take me to make the $239,000?"

"Eleven months"

"And how much of the $42,000 would I have to pay you up front?"

"Nothing. Just pay me as you start making the money using the system"

I watched it click. My dad got it. "Oh," he said, "well then, yeah, I would do it."

"And that's why they do it, too."

***

Making shit loads of money breaks people's minds. It literally stretches their minds so far past what they believe is possible they assume you are doing something wrong or illegal. They literally "can't even."

Why? Because they think to themselves . . . *they can't be that much smarter than me or work that much harder than me, so how is it possible for them to make 1,000 times more than me? Enough money that it would take me literally ten lifetimes to make what they make in a year.*

In the three years leading up to me writing this book, I took home over $1,200,000/mo in profit. Every. Single. Month. That's more than the compensation for the CEOs of Ford, McDonalds, Motorola, & Yahoo . . . combined . . . every year . . . as a kid in his twenties.

It angers those who believe life isn't fair. It confuses others who cannot comprehend and believe there must have been a mistake. And it inspires a select few, who are bound for greatness.

I hope that you are in the last category, because that is who I am writing this for.

You *can* do this.

You just need to learn *how*.

And I'm gonna show you.

Price to Value Discrepancy

"I hope what you're giving them is worth it."

Those words would probably sting for most, but when my dad said them to me, I just knew he didn't understand the *value* we were providing. What I want to show you is how to create and communicate value, aka the "worth-it-ness" of an offer.

In order to understand how to make a compelling offer, you must understand *value*. The reason people buy *anything* is to get a *deal*. They believe what they are getting (VALUE) is worth *more* than what they are giving in exchange for it (PRICE). The moment the value they receive dips below what they are paying, they stop buying from you. This price to value discrepancy is what you need to avoid at all costs.

After all, as Warren Buffet said, "Price is what you pay. Value is what you get."

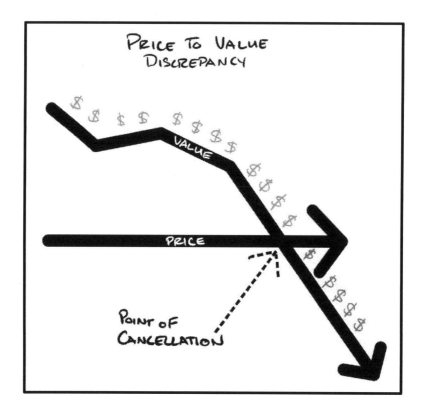

The simplest way to increase the gap between price to value is by lowering the price. It's also, most of the time, the wrong decision for the business.

Getting people to buy is NOT the objective of a business. Making money is. And lowering price is a one-way road to destruction for most — you can only go down to $0, but you can go infinitely high in the other direction. So, unless you have a revolutionary way of decreasing your costs to 1/10th compared to your competition, don't compete on price.

As Dan Kennedy said, "There is no strategic benefit to being the second cheapest in the marketplace, but there is for being the most expensive."

So the goal of our Grand Slam Offer will be to get more people to say yes *at a higher price* by increasing our value to price discrepancy. In other words, we will raise our price only *after* we have sufficiently increased our value. This way, they still get a great deal (think buying $100,000 of value for $10,000). It's 'money at a discount.'

FREE GIFT #3: BONUS TUTORIAL & FREE DOWNLOADS: Charge What It's Worth

If you want to know how I create value discrepancies for B2B or B2C products, go to **Acquisition.com/training/offers** course then watch **"Charge What It's Worth"** for a short video tutorial. My goal is to gain your trust and deliver value in advance. As such, it's absolutely free. Enjoy.

Why You Should Charge So Much It Hurts

Most business owners are *not* competing on price or value. In fact, they're not actually competing on anything at all. Their pricing process typically goes something like this:

1) Look at marketplace

2) See what everyone else offers

3) Take the average

4) Go slightly below to remain "competitive"

5) Provide what their competitors offers with a "little more"

6) End up at a value proposition of "more for less"

And the big secret: those competitors they are copying are dead broke. *So why on earth copy them?*

Pricing where the market is means you're pricing for market *efficiency*. Over time, in an efficient marketplace, more competitors enter offering "a little more for a little less," until eventually no one can provide any more for any less. At this point, a market reaches perfect efficiency, and the business owners participating make *just enough* at the end of the month to keep going. The bottom 10-20 percent of operators get washed out or lose the will to fight. Then fresh business owners enter with no idea and repeat the process of their forefathers. And around and around they go.

In plain words, pricing this way means you are providing a service at just above what it costs for you to stay above water. We are *not* trying to stay barely above water. We are trying to make egregious amounts of money that will have your relatives asking if what you are doing is legal. Again, we are not trying to get the most customers. <u>We are trying to make the most money</u>.

That being said, since there is no strategic benefit to being the second-lowest priced player in your marketplace. Allow me to give you a brief overview of why I see premium pricing as not only a very smart business decision, but a moral one. Furthermore, it's the only choice that will allow you to truly provide the most value, a unique and strong position in the marketplace. Let me introduce you to the virtuous cycle of price.

Virtuous Cycle of Price

3k | VIRTUOUS VS. VICIOUS CYCLE OF PRICE $

↓ PRICE	YOUR CLIENTS	PRICE ↑
DECREASE	EMOTIONAL INVESTMENT	INCREASE
DECREASE	PERCEIVED VALUE	INCREASE
DECREASE	RESULTS	INCREASE
INCREASE	DEMANDINGENESS	DECREASE
DECREASE	REVENUE FOR FULFILLMENT PER CUSTOMER	INCREASE

↓ PRICE	YOUR BUSINESS	PRICE ↑
DECREASE	PROFIT	INCREASE
DECREASE	PERCEIVED VALUE OF SELF	INCREASE
DECREASE	PERCEPTION OF IMPACT (RESULTS)	INCREASE
DECREASE	SERVICE LEVELS	INCREASE
DECREASE	SALES TEAM CONVICTION	INCREASE

I have used this framework in most of the materials I release because it needs to be consistently reinforced. The forces of the marketplace will grate on your belief system. You must stay strong and ignore them! Here's the basic premise of why you *need* to charge a premium if you want to best serve your customers.

When you decrease your price, you . . .

. . . Decrease your clients' emotional investment since it didn't cost them much

. . . Decrease your clients' perceived value of your service since it can't be that good if it's so cheap, or priced the same as everyone else

. . . Decrease your clients results because they do not value your service and are not invested

. . . Attract the worst clients who are *never* satisfied until your service is *free*

. . . Destroy any margin you have left to be able to actually provide an exceptional experience, hire the best people, invest in your people, pamper your clients, invest in growth, invest in more locations or more scale, and everything else that you had hoped in the goal of helping more people solve whatever problem it is that you solve.

In essence, your world sucks. And to make matters worse, your service probably sucks because you are squeezing blood from the proverbial stone. There's just not enough money left over to make something exceptional. As a result, you fall in line with the armies of average businesses that race to the bottom. I've lived that life. It's terrible. If you love your customers and your employees, please stop short-changing them when there is a better way.

Here's the reverse. This is what happens when you raise your prices.

When you raise your prices, you . . .

. . . *Increase* your clients' emotional investment

. . . *Increase* your clients' perceived value of your service

. . . *Increase* your clients' results because they value your service and are invested

. . . Attract the *best* clients who are *the easiest* to satisfy and actually cost *less* to fulfill, and who are the most likely to actually receive and perceive the most relative value

. . . *Multiply* your margin because you have money to *invest* in systems to create efficiency; smart people; improved customer experience; scale your business; and, most importantly of all, to keep watching the number in your personal bank account go up, month after month, even with reinvesting in your business. This allows you to ultimately enjoy the process for the long haul and help more people as you grow, rather than burning out and shriveling into obscurity.

To swing the argument even further in favor of higher prices, here are a few interesting concepts. When you raise your price, you increase the value the consumer receives without changing anything else about your product. Wait, what? Yes.

Higher Price Means Higher Value (Literally)

In a blind taste test, researchers asked consumers to rate three wines: a low-priced wine, a medium-priced wine and an expensive wine. Throughout the study, the participants rated the wines with the prices visible. They rated them, unsurprisingly, in order of their price, with the most expensive being the "best," the second most expensive being "second best," and the third, cheapest option, being rated as "cheap wine."

What the tasters didn't know is that the researchers gave them the exact same wine all three times. Yet, the tasters reported a wide discrepancy between the "high priced" wine and the "cheap" wine. This has deep implications for the direct relationship between value and price.

In essence, raising your prices can directly enhance the value you provide. What's more, the higher the price, the more allure your product or service has. People *want* to buy expensive things. They just need a reason. And the goal isn't just to be slightly above the market price — the goal is to be so much higher that a consumer thinks to themselves, "This is so much more expensive, there must be something entirely different going on here."

That is how you create a category of one. In this new perceived marketplace, you are a monopoly and can make monopoly profits. That is the point.

One final point I want to drive home: if you offer a service where a customer must do something in order to achieve the result, or solve the problem you say you solve, they must be invested. The more invested they are, the more likely they are to achieve the positive result. Therefore, it follows that if you care about your customers, you should get them as invested as humanly possible. Ideally, this means pricing your services or product in such a way that it *stings* a little when they buy. That sting will force and focus their attention and their investment in your product or service. Those who pay the most, pay the most attention. And if your customers are more adherent and follow through, and if they achieve better results with your service than your competition, then you are in a very real way providing more value than anyone else. This is how you win.

But I know this isn't easy, and it shouldn't be. Your product must *deliver.* So many wish to shortcut the real work. Do that and you *will* fail. In the real world, to have the "gonads" to charge big ticket prices, you must *outwork your self doubt.* You must be so confident in your delivery, because you have done it *so many times,* that you *know* that this person will succeed. Experience is what gives you the conviction to ask for someone's entire year's salary as payment. You must believe so deeply in your solution that when you look at yourself in the mirror at night, alone, your conviction remains unshakable. So let me bring this section home with my personal experience.

My Premium Price Experience

In my first niche consulting business — Gym Launch — I teach gym owners a better business model. Before productizing my consulting services, I flew out to 33 gyms in 18 months to do full turnarounds.

We would fly out, fix everything in the gym, and relaunch it in 21 days. We would average an increase in $42,000 in additional sales in 21 days. It was wild. My fee was the 100% of the revenue I would bring in.

At our peak, we were turning around eight gyms a month. This quickly became a logistical nightmare. After the wear and tear of living in motels month after month after month, I thought to myself *there has to be a better way to do this.*

One month, there was a gym we were scheduled to go fly out to. But, I simply didn't want to do it. So I told them we were going to cancel the engagement. The gym owner practically threatened me to help him. So I said I would help him, but he would have to do all the work, but I would show him how.

Within thirty days, this gym had made almost $44,000 in new up front cash collected sales (4x their previous month). As soon as I saw that my process could be duplicated from afar, without me having to fly people in. . .our business exploded. I had found the missing link because my travel schedule was no longer a constraint. We went on to sell 4000+ more gyms over the next few years (and counting) using a *done-with-you* rather than a *done-for-you* model. But. . .back to premium pricing.

When I entered the space, low-price competitors offered full-service marketing for $500 per month, with a single high-price competitor charging $5,000 for his product.

I wanted to be the premium price leader. I wanted to be so expensive that it created allure around what we were doing. So, we came in at three-times the highest-priced player and 32 times more than the lower-priced players. A price of $16,000 for a 16-week, done-with-you intensive. Then we upsold 35 percent of those people into a three-year, $42,000/year agreement for us to help them grow their gyms.

For context: The average gym owner makes $35,280/year in take-home profits. If that's the average, it means *half* make even *less* than that. So for many of them, they were committing to *half* of their yearly pay *or more* to buy our program. And I was selling this to grown men as a kid in his twenties, telling them I was going to help them make more money. This was possible because my conviction was stronger than their skepticism. *How?*

Based a voluntary survey taken at our last full company event, with 158 gyms responding, we found that a Gym Launch gym who has been in our program for 11 months will experience the following average improvements:

Top Line Revenue Growth: +$19,932/mo (+$239,000/yr)

Recurring Revenue Growth: +$13,339/mo (+$160,068/yr)

Bottom Line Growth (Profit): From $2,943/mo to $8,940/mo (3.1x!)

Client Growth: +67

Churn (% of clients who leave each month): From 10.7 percent to 6.8 percent

Retail Sales: +$4,400/mo in retail product sales revenue

Prices: From $129/mo to $167/mo

The survey just proved what I already knew. I had complete conviction in our product. I knew it worked. I had *outworked my self-doubt.*

Summary Points

What should you take from this?

First and foremost, charge a premium. It will allow you to do things no one else can to make your clients successful. We were able to charge a premium because we provided more value than anyone else in the industry. In a real way, we were charging on a *fraction* of what our clients made using our system. This is important. <u>Our clients still got a *deal*</u>. The gap between what they paid (price) and what they got (value) was massive. As a result, the virtuous cycle continued to spin. We charged the most money. We provided the most value.

Our gyms remained the most competitive, made the most money, always had the latest and best acquisition systems, and had the support to implement them at lightning speed.

We made many mistakes along the way, but our pricing model was not one of them. It allowed me the room to make big bets without losing the farm. The truth is that 99 percent of businesses need to raise their prices to grow, not lower them. Profit is oxygen. It fuels the fire of growth. You need it if you want to reach more people and make a bigger impact.

In order to charge so much, though, you must learn to create tremendous value. Let's head there next.

SECTION III
Value - Create Your Offer

How To Make Offers So Good People Feel Stupid Saying No

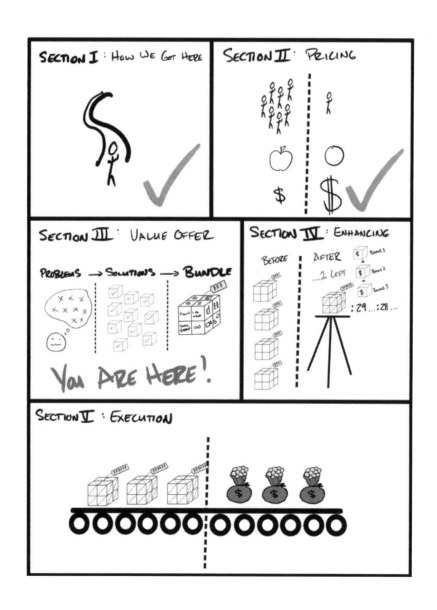

Value Offer: The Value Equation

"We question all of our beliefs, except for the ones we really believe in, and those we never think to question."

- Orson Scott Card

I want to be abundantly clear: the goal should be to charge as much money for your products or services as humanly possible. I'm talking heinous amounts of money. That being said, anyone can raise their prices, but only a select few can charge these rates *and get people to say yes.*

From this point forward, you must abandon any notion you have about "what's fair." Every enormous company in the world charges you money for things that cost them nothing. It costs pennies for the phone company to add an additional user, except they don't mind charging you hundreds per month for access. It costs pennies to manufacture pharmaceutical drugs, but they don't mind charging hundreds of dollars a month for it. Media companies charge advertisers a king's ransom for your eyeballs, and it costs them next to nothing to get you to like kitten photos on social media. You *need* to have a big discrepancy between what something costs you and what you charge for it. It is the only way to be unreasonably successful.

Many entrepreneurs believe that charging "too much" is bad. The reality is that, yes, you should never charge more than your product is *worth*. But you should charge *far* more for your product and services than it costs to fulfill it. Think up to a hundred times more, not just two or three times more. And if you provide enough *value*, it should still always be a *steal* for the prospect. That is the power of value. It unleashes unlimited pricing and profit power to scale your company.

For example, one of my private clients (whose company I have equity in) is in the photography space. Over two years, implementing the tactics outlined in this book, the owner was able to increase the average ticket from $300 to $1,500. That's a 5x increase (gasp). Even cooler, they now spend less time per customer, and have *higher* customer satisfaction. The 5x increase in average ticket, 38x'd the profit of the business. It went from making $1,000/wk in profit to $38,000/wk in profit, and continues to grow. As a result, the company was finally able to continue to scale to multiple locations and provide meaningful work to great employees. And a fun benefit, we were able to donate even more money to children's charities which is something the owner and I have in common (almost $500,000 at the time of this writing). But none of that would have been possible without figuring out what people valued most, tripling down on it, and ruthlessly eliminating everything else. A 5x price increase may seem crazy to you, but clients voted with their dollars that what the company provides now is *far* better than what it did before. Cracking value opens up the world of unlimited profit, impact and possibilities.

Those who understand *value* are the ones who will be able to charge the most money for their services. The good news is that there is a repeatable formula that I have created (I've never seen it displayed elsewhere) to help quantify the variables that create value for any offer. I call it *The Value Equation*. Once you see it, you can never unsee it. It will operate in your subconscious, running in the background, calling out to you. It's a new lens through which to see the world.

The Value Equation

```
┌ ─ ─ ─ ─ ─ ─ ─ ─ ─ ─ ─ ─ ─ ─ ─ ─ ─ ─ ─ ─ ─ ─ ─ ─ ─ ─ ─ ─ ┐
```
FREE GIFT #4: Value Equation Bonus Tutorial & Free Download(s):

If you want to know how I break down a businesses core offering into something more valuable go to **acquisition.com/offers** and select the **"Value Equation"** video to watch a short tutorial. I also included a downloadable checklist. My goal is to *gain your trust* and deliver value in advance. As such, it's absolutely free. Enjoy.
```
└ ─ ─ ─ ─ ─ ─ ─ ─ ─ ─ ─ ─ ─ ─ ─ ─ ─ ─ ─ ─ ─ ─ ─ ─ ─ ─ ─ ─ ┘
```

As you can see from the picture, there are four primary drivers of value. Two of the drivers (on top), you will seek to increase. The other two (on the bottom), you will seek to decrease.

(1) (Yay) The Dream Outcome (Goal: Increase)

(2) (Yay) Perceived Likelihood of Achievement (Goal: Increase)

(3) (Boo) Perceived Time Delay Between Start and Achievement (Goal: Decrease)

(4) (Boo) Perceived Effort & Sacrifice (Goal: Decrease)

If you noticed the questions in the last section that my father asked me, you'll see they corresponded with these pillars:

What will I make? (Dream Outcome)

How will I know it's going to happen? (Perceived Likelihood of Achievement)

How long will it take? (Time Delay)

What is expected of me? (Effort & Sacrifice)

Get The Bottom To Zero

In the beginning of my career, I focused all my attention on dream outcomes and the perception of achievement (social proof, third-party edification, etc). In other words, the top side of the equation. That's where beginner marketers make bigger and bigger claims. It's easy, and it's lazy.

But as time has gone on, I have realized that these larger-than-life claims are the easiest to establish (and therefore less unique). After all, anyone can make a promise. The harder, and more competitive, are the Time Delay and Effort & Sacrifice. The best companies in the world focus all their attention on the bottom side of the equation. Making things immediate, seamless, and effortless. Apple made the iPhone effortless compared to other phones at the time. Amazon made purchasing a single click of a button *and* made purchases arrive almost immediately (maybe by the time you read this, they'll be sending drones to our doors within 60 minutes). Netflix made consuming television immediate and effortless. So, the older I get, the more I have shifted my focus to "the hard stuff" — decreasing the bottom side of the equation. And I believe the better you do this, the more you will be rewarded by the marketplace.

Final note: The reason this is a division equation and not an addition ("+") is that I wanted to convey one key point. If you can make the bottom part of the equation equal to zero, you're golden. No matter how small the top side is, anything divided by zero equals infinity (which is technically undefined for the math nerds). In other words, if you can reduce your prospects' true time delay to receiving value to zero (aka you realize your immediate dream outcome), and your effort and sacrifice is zero, you have an infinitely valuable product. If you accomplish this, you win the game.

Given this postulate, a prospect would (in theory) purchase something from you, and the moment their credit card was run, it would immediately become their reality. *That* is infinite value.

Imagine clicking the purchase button on a weight loss product and instantly seeing your stomach turn into a six-pack. Or imagine hiring a marketing firm, and as soon as you sign your document, your phone begins ringing with new highly qualified prospects. How valuable would these products/services be? Infinitely valuable. And that's the point.

I don't know if we entrepreneurs will ever get there, but that is the hypothetical limit we all should strive towards, and why I structured the equation this way.

Perception is Reality

Perception is reality. It's not about how much you increase your prospect's likelihood of success, or decrease the time delay to achievement, or decrease their effort and sacrifice. That in itself is *not* valuable. Many times, they will have no idea. The Grand Slam Offer only becomes valuable once the prospect *perceives* the increase in likelihood of achievement, *perceives* the decrease in time delay, and *perceives* the decrease in effort and sacrifice.

A prime example of this happened in the London tunnel system. The biggest increase in rider satisfaction (*aka value*) was never from faster trains to decrease wait times. Instead, it was from a simple dotted map that showed them when the next train was coming and how long they had to wait. The dotted map, which only cost a few million dollars, decreased the riders' *perception* of time delay and sacrifice (being bored waiting) more than actually making the trains faster (which costs billions of dollars to do). Isn't that cool? This is how we need to think about our products.

Pro Tip: Logical vs Psychological Solutions

Most people naturally try and solve problems using *logical* solutions. But the logical solutions have usually been tried...because they're logical (it's what everyone would try and do).

As a business owners and entrepreneurs I increasingly approach problems to find *psychological* solutions, rather than *logical* ones. Because if there were a logical solution, it probably would have already been solved, thereby eliminating the problem. All that's left are the *psychological* problems.

Examples inspired by Rory Sutherland, CMO of Ogilvy Advertising:

"Any fool can sell a product by offering it for a discount, it takes great marketing to sell the same product for a premium"

Logical solution: make trains faster to increase satisfaction

Psychological solution: decrease the pain of waiting by adding a dotted map

Psychological solution: pay models to be the hostesses on the trip (people would wish it took longer to get to their destination!)

Logical solution: make elevator faster

Psychological solution: add floor to ceiling mirrors so people are distracted staring at themselves and forget how long they were on the elevator

Logical solution: make it cheaper

Psychological solution: make fewer of them and raise the price which causes people to want it more.

Often, most logical solutions have been tried and failed. At this point in history, we must give the psychological solutions a shot to solve problems.

As such, as business owners, it is up to us to communicate these value drivers with clarity to increase the prospect's perception of these realities. The extent to which you answer these questions in the mind of your prospect will determine the value you are creating. Only then, will we truly be able to realize the actual value of our product to the marketplace, and by extension, the egregious prices we want to charge.

It's difficult to separate the four value drivers from another, as most vehicles combine many of these elements together, but I will do my best to isolate and clearly explain each below.

#1 Dream Outcome (Goal = Increase)

People have deep, unchanging desires. This is what marriages are lost over, wars are fought over, and people will willingly die for. Our goal is not to create desire. It's simply to channel that desire through our offer and monetization vehicle.

The dream outcome is the expression of the feelings and experiences the prospect has envisioned in their mind. It's the gap between their current reality and their dreams. Our goal is to accurately depict that dream back to them, so they feel understood, and explain how our vehicle will get them there.

The dream outcome is simple; it's the "getting there" where the value gets enhanced or detracted.

People generally, and our clients specifically, want:

. . . To be perceived as beautiful

. . . To be respected

. . . To be perceived as powerful

. . . To be loved

. . . To increase their *status*

These are all powerful drivers.

But multiple vehicles may accomplish the same thing. Take the desire *"to be perceived as beautiful"* for example, here are a lot of things that touch on this desire:

Make Up

Anti-aging creams/serums

Supplements

Shapewear

Plastic Surgery

Fitness

→ All these vehicles channel the desire to be perceived as beautiful.

And if we further unpack the idea of a desire to be beautiful, we see that it may be a surface-level declaration of a deeper desire to achieve higher status in one's social group.

The dream outcome value driver is most prominently used when comparing the relative value *between two different desires being satisfied*. In general, the dream outcome that most directly increases a prospect's status will be the one they value most. As such, a prospect may value that entire category of vehicles that satisfy one desire more than another category that satisfies a different desire. For many men, making money is more important than being handsome. Why? Because money drives status for men more than being handsome does. So, in general, they will value all offers that make them money more than offers that help them look good.

I once heard Russell Brunson tell a story about this concept. He explained how his wife, Collette, at first hearing about this status concept, rejected it. She claimed she wasn't driven by status and would never want to drive a Lamborghini. Instead, she favored her minivan. But, after talking further, she revealed it was because driving a Lamborghini would decrease her status amongst her mom friends, while driving a minivan would show she was a good mother (increase in status). So it's not about the money, it's about the *status (the perceived increase or decrease in relative standing when compared to others socially or professionally)*. Talk in terms of things your prospect believes will increase their status, and you will have your prospects drooling.

Pro Tip: Frame benefits in terms of status gained *from the viewpoint of others*

When writing copy, you can make it that much more powerful by talking about how *other people* will perceive the prospect's achievement. Connect the dots for them. Example: If you buy this golf club, your drive will increase by 40 yards. Your golf buddies' jaws will drop when they see your ball soar 40 yards past theirs . . . they'll ask you what's changed . . . only you will know.

That being said, when comparing two products or services that satisfy the *same* desire, the value from the dream outcomes will cancel out (since they are the same). It will be the other three variables that drive the difference in perceived value, and ultimately price. For example, if we have two products or services that both help make someone beautiful, it will be the likelihood of achievement, time delay, and effort required that will differentiate the perceived value of each offer.

Simply put: if two things make someone beautiful, what makes one worth $50,000 and another $5? Answer: The extent of the other three value variables.

#2 Perceived Likelihood of Achievement (Goal = Increase)

This was the last of the variables I added when trying to think through this framework a few years ago. I just felt like something was missing with only the other three.

Then I realized people pay for certainty. They value certainty. I call this "the perceived likelihood of achievement." In other words, "How likely do I believe it is that I will achieve the result I am looking for if I make this purchase?"

For example, how much would you pay to be a plastic surgeon's 10,000th patient versus their first?

If you're a normal, sane person, a lot more. I mean heck, you might even ask them to pay you if you are their first patient ever.

So you can see even from this simple example that while the service you are receiving is technically the same, the only thing that changes is your perceived likelihood of getting what you want.

Both surgeons take the same amount of time to do the surgery (if anything, the guy who has done it 10,000 times would likely get it done faster and *still* charge *more*). The more-experienced surgeon has a track record of achieving a result, which incentivizes their desirability.

People value this perceived likelihood of achievement. Increasing a prospect's conviction that your offer will "actually" work for them, will make your offer that much more valuable even though the work remains the same on your end. So to increase value with all offers, we must communicate perceived likelihood of achievement through our messaging, proof, what we choose to include or exclude in our offer, and our guarantees (more on these later).

#3 Time Delay (Goal = Decrease)

Time delay is the time between a client buying and receiving the promised benefit. The shorter the distance between when they purchase and they receive value/the outcome, the more valuable your services or product is.

There are two elements to this driver of value: Long-term outcome and short-term experience. Many times, there are short-term experiences that occur while en route to the long-term outcomes. They happen "along the way" and provide value.

It's good to understand both. The thing people *buy* is the long-term value, aka their "dream outcome." But the thing that makes them *stay* long enough to get it is the short-term experience. These are little milestones a prospect sees along the way that shows them they are on the right path. We try and tie as many of these as possible into any service we offer. We want clients to have a big emotional win early (as close as possible to their purchase). This gives them the emotional buy in and the momentum to "see it through" to their ultimate goal.

For example, it takes a while to add an extra $239,000 per year to a gym. But that's what they're buying. So, once they have purchased, we need to create emotional wins fast. One way we do this is to get their ads live and get them to close their first $2,000 sale within their first seven days. By doing this, their decision to work with us is reinforced, and they immediately trust us more. This makes them more likely to follow the rest of our systems and get to their ultimate destination.

Pro Tip: Fast Wins

Always try and incorporate short-term, immediate wins for a client. Be creative. They just need to know they are on the right path and that they made the right decision trusting you and your business.

Let me give you another example. If I sell someone a bikini body, their time delay to realize that outcome may be 12 months or even longer. Along the way, though, as they change their bodies, they may experience higher sex drive, more energy, and an increased community of friends.

They aren't *initially* buying those things, but those things may become short-term benefits that keep them in the game long enough to achieve their ultimate outcome. They buy the dream, but they stay for the benefits they discover along the way. The faster and more clearly you can demonstrate those benefits, the more valuable your service will be. For a weight loss customer, we would get them to meet someone else so they immediately had some social benefits from the program, *and* we usually gave them a more aggressive diet in the beginning. Why? Because we wanted them to have a big, fast emotional win, so we could get them to commit to the long term. This is also backed by science. People who experience a victory early on are more likely to continue with something than those who do not.

That being said, having to wait 12 to 24 months to get what you want is a *long* time when you can do liposuction and be done in an afternoon. This shows just one of the reasons people pay $25,000 for liposuction with a tummy tuck, while people will barely pay $100/mo to join a bootcamp.

But that's not the only reason, is it?

That leads me to the last driver of value - effort and sacrifice.

Pro Tip: Fast Beats Free

The only thing that beats "free" is "fast." People will pay for speed. Many companies have entered free spaces and done exceedingly well with a "speed first" strategy. A few notable examples: The MVD vs DMV wait in line forever or pay $50 you can skip the line and get your license renewed privately. Fedex vs USPS (when it absolutely positively has to be there overnight). Spotify vs Slow Free Music. Uber vs Walking. Fast beats free. Many will always be willing to pay (price) for the (value) of speed. So if you find yourself in a market competing against free, double down on speed.

#4 Effort & Sacrifice (Goal = Decrease)

This is what it "costs" people in ancillary costs, aka "other costs accrued along the way." These can be both tangible and intangible.

Using the fitness versus liposuction example, let's look at the difference in effort and sacrifice:

Fitness Effort and Sacrifice:	liposuction effort and sacrifice:
Wake up one to two hours earlier in the morning	Fall asleep
Five to ten hours per week of time lost	Wake up thin, guaranteed
Stop eating the foods you love	Be sore for two to four weeks
Constant hunger	
Physical soreness	
Feelings of embarrassment at not knowing how to exercise	
Risk of injury	
Actual nausea working out	
Meal prepping	
New groceries/more expensive	
New clothing (can be a benefit for some folks)	
Fear of gaining it back after all this effort (impermanence)	
Etc . . .	

Massive difference, right?

In fact, in looking at the marketing of plastic surgeons, these are the *exact* pain points they hit on when they say things like: *"Tired of wasting countless hours in the gym. . . . tired of trying diets that just don't work?"*

This is why when you sell fitness, you have to spend an hour arm-wrestling a client to give over 1/10th to 1/100th of the amount of money they pay for surgery. There's just not a lot of perceived value because the perceived likelihood of achievement, the time delay to achievement, and the effort and sacrifice are so high.

So even though the outcome is the same, the value of the vehicles are dramatically different, hence the difference in price.

Decreasing the effort and sacrifice, or at least the perceived effort and sacrifice, can massively boost the appeal of your offer.

In an ideal world, a prospect would want to simply "say yes" and have their dream outcome happen with no more effort on their behalf.

This is why "done for you services" are almost always more expensive than "do-it-yourself" because the person doesn't have all the effort and sacrifice. There is also a component of "perceived likelihood of achievement" difference as well. People believe that if an expert does it, then they will be more likely to achieve the outcome than if they try on their own.

My hope is that you now have a foundational understanding of the components of value and how the interplay between each of the components creates or detracts from the value someone might be willing to pay.

Putting It All Together

As I said earlier, these elements of value don't happen in a vacuum. They happen together, in combination. So let's look at a few examples that utilize all four components of value at once.

In an effort to quantify the value, I'll rate them on a binary scale of 0 or 1. 1 being value achieved. 0 being missing. Then I will add all four together to give you a relative value rating of a type of service. Our goal as marketers and business owners is to *increase* the value of the dream outcome and its perceived likelihood of achievement, while *decreasing* the time delay of achievement and the effort and sacrifice one has to put in to get there.

To start I will do a side by side comparison of two "vehicles" with identical Dream outcomes: Meditation and Xanax. Both offer the buyer relaxation, decreased anxiety, and feelings of well-being. I will demonstrate how the other three variables dramatically shift the value of delivering that dream outcome and ultimately, the price.

Example: Dream Outcome: "Relaxation," "Decreased Anxiety," "Feelings of well-being" *Meditation vs Xanax*

Value Measure	Meditation	Score	Xanax	Score
Dream Outcome	"Relaxation" "Decreased Anxiety" "Feelings of well-being"	1/1	"Relaxation" "Decreased Anxiety" "Feelings of well-being"	1/1
Perceived Likelihood	Low, since most people get distracted and don't actually think they'll follow through with daily meditation	0/1	High, since most people are confident that if they take the pill, it will make them feel more relaxed	1/1
Time Delay	Long time to yield long term results. Some immediate benefits after 10 to 20 minutes (assuming you don't get frustrated)	.5/1	15 minutes for effects to be felt	1/1
Effort & Sacrifice	Physical discomfort (numb body limbs often). Mental discomfort (feeling like you are failing at it constantly). Time sacrifice (you have to set time aside everyday to do it).	0/1	Swallowing the pill	1/1
Overall Value	**Low**	1.5/4	**High**	4/4

And that is why Xanax is a multi-billion dollar product while I know of almost no multi-billion dollar meditation businesses . . . value.

I'm not here to argue about whether meditation is better than Xanax (obviously it is) but that doesn't mean it's perceived as more valuable.

This is also the reason that the supplement industry ($123B, *Grandview Research*) is twice the size of the health club industry ($62B, *IHRSA*). They both accomplish the same perceived objectives — "being healthy," "losing weight," "looking good," "increased energy," etc. — but one is perceived as more valuable because it has lower "costs."

People are more willing to pay $200 for supplements than they are a $29/mo membership. Taking a pill, or drinking a shake, is so much faster and easier than going to the gym everyday. Hence . . . valued.

Crazy world we live in.

And you can either sit there and make "complain" posts about how people "ought" to be a certain way. Or you can take advantage of the way people *are* and capitalize. This book is for those people who want to be victors, not victims of circumstances.

You can either be right or you can be rich. This book is for getting rich. If that bothers you, just put this down and go back to arguing against human nature. Hint: You're not gonna change it.

Now, that being said, knowing what people value versus what is good for them is key. It means you can find ways to monetize the things that people value in order to give them what they really need.

Win-win.

You can make your dent in the universe *while* making a profit.

Free Goodwill

"He who said money can't buy happiness, hasn't given enough away."

- Unknown

People who help others (with zero expectation) experience higher levels of fulfillment, live longer, *and* make more money. I'd like to create the opportunity to deliver this value to you during your reading or listening experience. In order to do so, I have a simple question for you...

Would you help someone you've never met, if it didn't cost you money, but you never got credit for it?

If so, I have an 'ask' to make on behalf of someone you do not know. And likely, never will.

They are just like you, or like you were a few years ago: less experienced, full of desire to help the world, seeking information but unsure where to look….this is where you come in.

The only way for us at acquisition.com to accomplish our mission of helping entrepreneurs is, first, by reaching them. And most people do, in fact, judge a book by its cover (and it's reviews). If you have found this book valuable thus far, would you please take a brief moment right now and leave an honest review of the book and its contents? It will cost you zero dollars and less than 60 seconds.

Your review will help….

….one more entrepreneur support his or her family.

….one more employee find work they find meaningful.

….one more client experience a transformation they otherwise would never have encountered.

….one more life change for the better.

To make that happen...all you have to do is….and this takes less than 60 seconds….leave a review.

If you are on audible - hit the three dots in the top right of your device, click rate & review, then leave a few sentences about the book with a star rating.

If you are reading on kindle or an e-reader - you can scroll to the bottom of the book, then swipe up and it will automatically prompt a review.

If for some reason they have changed either functionality - you can go to the book page on amazon (or wherever you purchased this) and leave a review right on the page.

PS - If you feel good about helping a faceless entrepreneur, you are my kind of people. I'm that much more excited to help you crush it in the coming chapters (you'll love the tactics I'm about to go over).

PPS - Life hack: if you introduce something valuable to someone, they associate that value with you. If you'd like goodwill directly from another entrepreneur - send this book their way.

Thank you from the bottom of my heart. Now back to our regularly scheduled programming.

- Your biggest fan, Alex

Value Offer: The Thought Process

"If at first you don't succeed, try, try, try again."

- Thomas H. Palmer, Teacher's Manual

I want to do an exercise with you right now. I want to show you the difference between convergent and divergent problem solving. Why? So that you can actually create the Grand Slam Offer that will become the cornerstones of your business.

Convergent & Divergent Thinking

In simple terms, convergent problem solving is where you take lots of variables, all known, with unchanging conditions and converge on a singular answer. Think math.

Example:

You have 3 salespeople who can each take 100 calls per month each.

It takes 4 calls to create one sale (including no shows).

You need to get to 110 sales . . .

How many sales people must you hire?

Deduced Information:

1 salesperson = 100 calls

4 calls = 1 close

100 calls/4 calls per close = 25 Closes Per 100 Calls

25 closes per rep

Goal: 110 sales *total* / 25 sales per rep = 4.4

Since you can't hire 4.4 reps, you decide you must have *five*.

ANSWER: And since you have 3, you hire *two* more.

Math problems are convergent. There are lots of variables and a single answer. We are taught all our lives in school to think this way. That is because it's easy to grade.

But life will pay you for your ability to solve using a divergent thought process. In other words, think of many solutions to a single problem. Not only that, convergent answers are binary. They are either right or they are wrong. With divergent thinking, you can have multiple right answers, and one answer that is way more right than the others. Cool right?

Here's what life presents us for divergent thinking: Multiple Variables, Known & Unknown, Dynamic Conditions, Multiple Answers.

As such, I want to do an exercise with you that will engage the part of your brain that you will need to use in order to make something magical.

I call it the "brick" exercise. Don't worry, it'll only take 120 seconds.

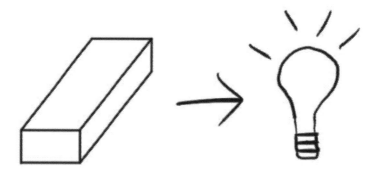

The Brick Exercise

Right now, I want you to set a timer on your phone for 120 seconds. What you need to do: Think of a brick.

Write down as many *different* uses of a brick as you can possibly think of. How many different ways could a brick be used in life to provide value.

Ready? Go. It's okay to write in the book.

_____

_____

_____

_____

_____

_____

_____

_____

_____

_____

_____

_____

_____

_____

_____

_____

_____

_____

_____

Alright — stop. Now before I show you my list, did you consider the following . . .

. . . How big is the brick? A tab of gum, 3-5/8" x 2-1/4" x 8" (Standard), 2 ft x 2 ft x 6ft?

. . . What is the brick made of? Plastic, Gold, Clay, Wood, Metal?

. . . How is the brick shaped? Does it have holes in it? Does it have divots for interlocking?

Now as you think about that, can you think of even more uses for the brick than you probably wrote down?

Here's my list:

— Paper weight

— Door stop

— Building things

— Home for a fish in a fish bowl

— Plant holder with dirt in the holes (holed brick)

— As a trophy (painted brick)

— Rustic decoration

— To break window

— Make a mural (tiny bricks painted)

— A weight for resistance training

— A wedge under uneven platform

— Pen holder (holed brick)

— Children's toy (lego bricks)

— Floatation device (plastic brick)

— Payment for goods (gold brick)

— Stabilizer for leaning something against

— Retainer of value (gold brick)

— Holder for flagpole (holed brick)

— A seat (jumbo brick)

Every offer has building blocks, the pieces that when combined make an offer irresistible. Our goal is to use a divergent thought process to think of as many easy ways to combine these elements to provide value.

So if I were selling a brick, I would find out what my customer's desire was, and then devise how many ways I could create value with my "brick."

Now let's do it for real.

Value Offer: Creating Your Grand Slam Offer Part I: Problems & Solutions

"ABC, Easy as 123 Ah, simple as doh reh mi"

- Michael Jackson, "ABC"

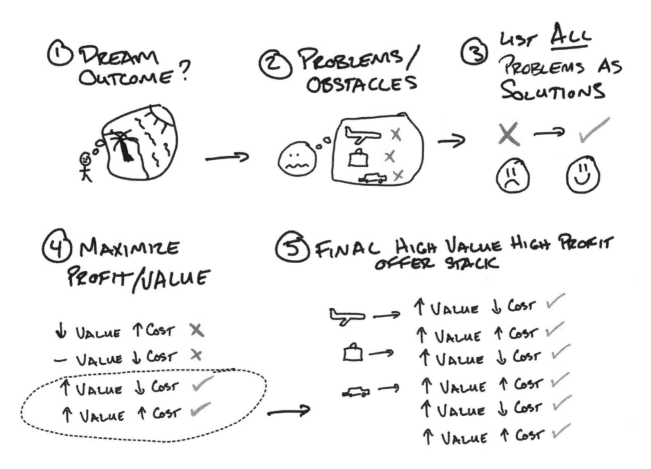

When I started my gym, I struggled. I wanted so deeply to be successful, prove my dad wrong about my decision to start my own business, and prove to myself that I was worth something. But try as I did, I couldn't even sell people into a $99/mo bootcamp. People would say, "LA Fitness is $29/mo. This is expensive." I even tried getting people to start for free. They said they wouldn't bother because $99/mo afterwards was still too much, and they didn't want to start something they wouldn't continue with.

It's a new level of frustration when you can't even give your services away for free to people. I felt worthless, and I didn't know what to do. Thankfully, during this time, I was in groups with other gym owners, and I started hearing about marketers and books. I devoured everything I could. And as soon as I stumbled on Dan Kennedy's books, I was hooked.

In his books, he talked about making "irresistible offers." Again, this theme of "making an offer so good people would feel stupid to say no" kept re-appearing. But this time, remembering what TJ had told me, I decided to go all in on this concept, rather than just do what everyone else was doing.

But how? Everyone else was selling $99/mo bootcamps. How was I going to compete? So I decided to look at what we did differently. I thought — what do they *really* want? No one wants a membership; they want to lose weight.

Step #1: Identify Dream Outcome

I had heard of weight loss challenges, so I started there.

Lose 20lbs in 6 weeks.

Big dream outcome - lose 20lbs.

With a decreased time delay - 6 weeks.

Note: I wasn't selling my membership anymore. I wasn't selling the plane flight. *I was selling the vacation.* When you are thinking about your dream outcome, it has to be them arriving at their destination and what they would like to *experience*.

Step #2: List Problems

Next, I wrote down all the things people struggled with and their limiting thoughts around them. When listing out problems, think about what happens immediately before and immediately after someone uses your product/service. What's the "next" thing they need help with? These are all the problems. Think about it in insane detail. If you do, you will create a more valuable and compelling offer as you'll continually be answering people's next problem as it manifests..

So, let's go ahead and list out the problems from a prospect's perspective as you think about them. What points of friction exist for them? I like to think in the sequence that the customer will experience each of these obstacles. Again, channel insane detail (the more problems the better!).

Example Problem List: Weight Loss

First thing they must do: Buying healthy food, grocery shopping

1) Buying healthy food is hard, confusing, and I won't like it

2) Buying healthy food will take too much time

3) Buying healthy food is expensive

4) I will not be able to cook healthy food forever. My family's needs will get in my way. If I travel I won't know what to get.

Next thing they must do: *Cooking healthy food*

1) Cooking healthy food is hard and confusing. I won't like it, and I will suck at it.

2) Cooking healthy food will take too much time

3) Cooking healthy food is expensive. It's not worth it.

4) I will not be able to buy healthy food forever. My family's needs will get in my way. If I travel I won't know how to cook healthy.

Next thing they must do: *Eating healthy food*

1) Etc...

Next thing they must do: *Exercise Regularly*

1) Etc...

Now we're gonna go full circle here. Each of the above problems has four negative elements. And you guessed it, each aligns with the four value drivers as well.

1) Dream Outcome→ This will not be financially worth it

2) Likelihood of Achievement→ It won't work for me specifically. I won't be able to stick with it. External factors will get in my way. (This is the most unique and service-specific of the problem buckets).

3) Effort & Sacrifice→ This will be too hard, confusing. I won't like it. I will suck at it.

4) Time→ This will take too much time to do. I am too busy to do this. It will take too long to work. It won't be convenient for me.

Now, go ahead and list out *all* the problems your prospect has. Don't let these buckets, which are just meant to get your brain going, constrain you. If it's easier for you, just list out everything you can possibly think of.

What I showed here isn't just four problems, though. We have 16 core problems with two to four sub problems underneath. So 32 to 64 problems total. Yowza. No wonder most people don't achieve their goals. Do not get overwhelmed. This is the best news ever. The more problems you think of, the more problems you get to solve.

So, to recap, just list out each core thing that someone has to do. Then think of all the reasons they wouldn't be able to do it, or keep doing it (using the four value drivers as a guide).

Now we get to the fun part: *turning problems into solutions*.

Step #3: Solutions List

Now that we have our dream outcome and all the obstacles that will get in someone's way, it's time to define our solutions and list them out.

Creating the solutions list has two steps. First, we are going to first transform our problems into solutions. Second, we are going to name these solutions. That's it. So let's take a look at our list of problems from earlier. What we're going to do is simply turn them into solutions by thinking, *"What would I need to show someone to solve this problem?"* Then we are going to reverse each element of the obstacle into solution-oriented language. This is copywriting 101. It's beyond the scope of this book to get into, but simply adding "how to" then reversing the problem will give most people new to this process a great place to start. For our purposes, we are giving ourselves a checklist of exactly what we are going to have to do for our prospects and what we are going to solve for them.

Once we have our list of solutions, we will operationalize how we are *actually* going to solve these problems (create value) in the next step. And I want to be 100 percent clear. You *will* solve every problem. We'll explore how together, in the next step.

PROBLEM→ SOLUTION

PROBLEM: Buying healthy food, grocery shopping

. . . is hard, confusing, I won't like it. I will suck at it→ How to make buying healthy food easy and enjoyable, so that anyone can do it (especially busy moms!)

. . . takes too much time→ How to buy healthy food quickly

. . . is expensive→ How to buy healthy food for less than your current grocery bill

. . . is unsustainable→ How to make buying healthy food take less effort than buying unhealthy food

. . . is not my priority. My family's needs will get in my way→ How to buy healthy food for you and your family at the same time

. . . is undoable if I travel; I won't know what to get→ How to get healthy food when traveling

PROBLEM: Cooking healthy food

. . . is hard, confusing. I won't like it, and I will suck at it→ How anyone can enjoy cooking healthy meals easily

. . . will take too much time→ How to cook meals in under 5 minutes

. . . is expensive, it's not worth it→ How eating healthy is actually cheaper than unhealthy food

. . . is unsustainable → How to make eating healthy last forever

. . . is not my priority, my family's needs will get in my way→ How to cook this despite your families concerns

. . . is undoable if I travel I won't know how to cook healthy→ How to travel and still cook healthy

PROBLEM: *Eating healthy food*

. . . is hard, confusing, and I won't like it→ How to eat delicious healthy food, without following complicated systems

. . . etc

PROBLEM: *Exercise Regularly*

. . . is hard, confusing, and I won't like it, and I will suck at it → Easy to follow exercise system that everyone enjoys

. . . .etc.

Okay, whew. That's a lot of problems (and a lot of intuited solutions courtesy of divergent thinking). You'll also notice that a lot of them are repetitive. That's totally normal. The value drivers are the four core reasons. Our problems always relate to those drivers, and our solutions provide the needed answer to give a prospect permission to purchase. What's even crazier: is that if *only one* of these needs is missing in a solution, it can cause someone *not* to buy. You would be *amazed* at the reasons people do not buy. So don't limit yourself here.

Brooke Castillo is a friend who runs an enormous life coaching business. To give you a different take on the problems-solutions list, Brooke sent me her list as she was going through this book to make a Grand Slam Offer for a 90-Day Relationship course. Take a look to see this process through a totally different lens. The main takeaway, though: Don't be fancy. Just get all the problems down then turn them into solutions.

Regardless of whether the offer you're creating is around fitness (like the example), a relationship course (like Brooke), or something wildly different (like ear aches), we now know *what* we need to do. Step four is the *how* (and how to do it without breaking the bank).

Dream Outcome →
Amazing, loving relationship in 90 days

Problems →
no good options
not attractive
not available
boring
no chemistry
poor communication
not hot enough
sex isnt good
no intellectual stimulation
not enough effort into relat
no time
insecurity
"needs" not met
too many unmet expectations
acting crazy emotional
relationship is dull
want different things
not good at relationships
too much pressure
moves too slow
fizzles out fast
kids involved
sexual incompatibility

Solutions List →

How to get a list of prospective
    partners to invite into 90 day
                        chosen
How to be attracted to your partner

How to find an available partner

How to make sure 90 day is
    exciting and never boring

How to create chemistry like you've
    never known

How to communicate in sexy, fun
    and meaningful ways

How to make the relationship hot
    by being hot

How to have great sex for 90 days

How to create intellectual stimulation

How to put the effort in the
    relationship for max return

How to make time for hourly
    dopamine/love hits

How to overcome all insecurity w/in
    the 90 day relationship

Value Offer: Creating Your Grand Slam Offer Part II: Trim & Stack

"Cut! Cut! Cut!"–Friends to Rachel Green in Friends

I divided this chapter into two parts because it's the meatiest section in the book. It's also the most important. Without a valuable product or service, the rest of the book won't be as actionable. We just covered all the problems we are going to solve. The second half of making your offer is breaking down tactically what we are going to do/provide for our client. In theory, we'd all love to fly out and live with our customers to fix their problems. In reality, that wouldn't make a very scalable business. We need our offer to be incredibly attractive *and* profitable.

That being said, if this is your first Grand Slam Offer, it's important to over-deliver like crazy. Maybe flying out isn't such a bad idea in the beginning. Make some sales, then think about how to make it easier for your clients. You want them to think to themselves, "I get all this, for only that?" In essence, you want them to perceive *tremendous value*.

Everyone buys bargains. Some people just buy $100,000 things for only $10,000. That's where we want to live: high prices, but a *steal* for the value (like hopefully this book so far).

Sales to Fulfillment Continuum

In order to best absorb the notions of trimming and stacking, we need a mental reframe. Enter the sales to fulfillment continuum.

Whenever you are building a business, you have a continuum between ease of fulfillment and ease of sales. If you lower what you have to do, it increases how hard your product or service is to sell. If you do as much as possible, it makes your product or service easy to sell but hard to fulfill because there's more demand on your time investment. The trick, and the ultimate goal, is to find a sweet spot where you sell something very well that's also easy to fulfill.

I have always lived by the mantra, "Create flow. Monetize flow. Then add friction." This means I generate demand *first*. Then, with my offer, I get them to say yes. Once I have people saying yes, then, and only then, will I add friction in my marketing, or decide to offer *less* for the same price.

Practicality drives this practice. If you can't get demand flowing in, then you have no idea whether what you have is good. I'd rather do more for every customer and have cash flow coming in, then optimize my business but have zero cash flow coming in after (and zero idea about what I need to adjust to better serve my customers).

Here's a perfect example to drive this home. When I started Gym Launch, gym owners reached out asking me to help. They needed so much help, I didn't know where to start. But I wanted to make sure they got way more than they paid me. So here's what I ended up doing to fill their gyms: I would fly out to their gym for 21 days, spend my own money on hotels, car rentals, eating out, advertising, generate the leads, work the leads, then sell for them. I would even do the first onboarding meeting with clients to get them started. In short, I did *everything*. I took on all the risk.

They only had to put down $500 to "reserve" their date, which I made refundable at the end of their launch. So they had 0 financial risk, 0 time risk, 0 effort, and the deal was, I got to keep all the up front cash collected from selling their services, and they got clients for free. You can imagine how this was a pretty compelling offer.

On my own, I was able to sell about $100,000/mo in up front cash for myself. So these deals were very lucrative for me. Over time, I scaled that to a team of 8 guys selling every month. But this began to wear on me and the team. It was at that point that I realized that if I were to simply teach them how to do what I did, I could charge maybe a third of what I would normally make, but I would be able to help hundreds of gyms a month instead of eight. And, I could do it all sleeping in my own bed every night.

My promise was fundamentally the same: I will fill your gym in 30 days. It was simply the *how* and *what I did* that changed. The *how and what* is what we are breaking apart.

When talking to business owners about their model, I tell them to create cash flow by over-delivering like crazy at first. Then use the cash flow to fix your operations and make your business more efficient. This revision process can be pretty seamless. You may not even have to change what you offer. You may just end up creating systems that create the same value for the customer but cost you significantly less resources.

Ultimately this is how businesses beat one another. Understanding this will be important as you scale your business.

Now that we've established the importance of the fulcrum and how to approach the sales-fulfillment balance at the outset, let's cover the last two steps of creating our Grand Slam offer. To recap quickly, remember that we covered identifying dream outcomes (step one), listing problems (step two), and determining solutions (step three).

Step #4 Create Your Solutions Delivery Vehicles ("The How")

The next step is thinking about all the things you could *do* to solve each of these problems you've identified. This is the most important step in this process. This is what you are going to *deliver*. This is what you are going to do or provide in exchange for money.

For the purposes of keeping creativity high (divergent thinking), think about *anything you could possibly do*. Think of all the things that might enhance the value of your offer. So much so that they would be stupid to say no.

What could you do that someone would immediately say, "All that? Seriously? Yes, I'm in."

Doing this exercise will make your job of selling So. Much. Easier.

Even if you come up with something you're not actually willing to do, it's okay. The goal here is to push your limits and jog your brain into thinking of a different version of the solution you'd normally default to. This is where you get to flex your entrepreneurial creativity.

Reminder: You only need to do this *once*. Literally *one time* for a product that may last years. This is high-value, high-leverage work. You ultimately get paid for *thinking*. You got this. This should be fun. Go ahead and list out all your possibilities now. Then I'll take you through my example. I'll just use the buying food problem from earlier as an example. I like to group things by how many people I'm going to deliver this thing to at once.

My list is below. And at the bottom, I've given you my "cheat codes" for how I think through this to get even more creative.

Problem: Buying Healthy Food Is Hard, Confusing, and I Won't Like It

If I wanted to provide a one-on-one solution I might offer . . .

a) In-person grocery shopping, where I take clients to the store and teach them how to shop

b) Personalized grocery list, where I teach them how to make their list

c) Full-service shopping, where I buy their food for them. We're talking 100 percent done for them.

d) In-person orientation (not at store), where I teach them what to get

e) Text support while shopping, where I help them if they get stuck

f) Phone call while grocery shopping, where I plan to call when they go shopping to provide direction and support

If I wanted to provide a small group solution I might offer . . .

a) In-person grocery shopping, where I meet a bunch of people and take them all shopping for themselves

b) Personalized grocery list, where I teach a bunch of people how to make their weekly lists. I could do this one time or every week if I wanted to.

c) Buy their food for them, where I purchase their groceries and deliver them as well

d) In-person orientation, where I teach a small group offsite what to do (not at store)

If I wanted to provide a one to many solution I might offer . . .

a) Live grocery tour virtual, where I might live stream me going through the grocery store for all my new customers and let them ask questions live

b) Recorded grocery tour, where I might shop once, record it, then give it as a reference point from that point onwards for my clients to watch on their own

c) DIY grocery calculator, where I create a shareable tool or show them how to use a tool to calculate their grocery list

d) Predetermined lists, where each customer plan comes with its own grocery list for each week. I could make this ahead of time so they have it. Then they could use it on their own time

e) Grocery buddy system, where I could pair customers all up, which takes no time really, and let them go shopping together

f) Pre-made, insta-cart grocery carts for delivery, where I could pre-make insta-cart lists so clients could have their groceries delivered to their doorstep with one click

As you see, the list can really go on and on here. This is just to illustrate the many ways to solve a *single* problem.

Now do this for *all* of the perceived problems that your clients encounter before, after, and during their experience with your service/products. You should have a monster list by the end of this.

Product Delivery Cheat Codes

What's that? You're having trouble being creative? I'm going to give you the cheat codes right now, kind of like I did with the brick example: "the brick could be gold, or plastic, or have holes in it, or be a lego, etc." Here are my "cheat codes" for product variation/enhancement and a visual to break down the process for you from my consulting deck:

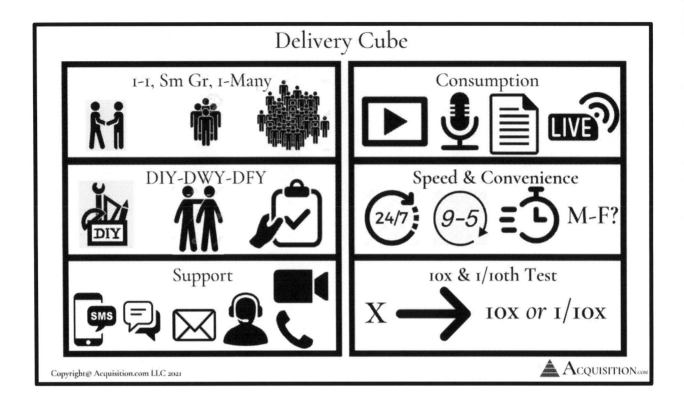

a) <u>What level of personal attention do I want to provide?</u> one-on-one, small group, one to many

b) <u>What level of effort is expected from them?</u> Do it themselves (DIY) - figure out how to do it on their own; do it with them (DWY) - you teach them how to do it; done for them (DFY) - you do it for them

c) <u>If doing something *live,* what environment or medium do I want to deliver it in?</u> In-person, phone support, email support, text support, Zoom support, chat support

d) <u>If doing a recording, how do I want them to consume it?</u> Audio, video, or written.

e) <u>How quickly do we want to reply? On what days? during what hours?</u> 24/7. 9-5, within 5 minutes, within an hour, within 24 hrs?

f) <u>10x to 1/10th test.</u> If my customers paid me 10x my price (or $100,000) what would I provide? If they paid me 1/10th the price and I had to make my product more valuable than it already is, how would I do that? How could I still make them successful for 1/10th price? Stretch your mind in either direction and you'll come up with widely different solutions.

In other words, how could I actually *deliver* on these solutions I am claiming I will provide. Do this for each problem because solutions from one problem will give you ideas for others you wouldn't normally have considered.

Remember, it's important that you solve *every* problem. I can't tell you the amount of times *one* single item becomes the reason someone doesn't buy.

Anecdote: Why We Must Solve *Every* Perceived Problem

When I was selling weight loss, I insisted that folks prepare all their food at home. I found it too difficult to help clients lose weight when they ate out because they always blew their diets. Rather than solve the problem, I insisted they do it my way, or not at all. As a result, I lost many sales.

One month I really needed to make some sales to pay rent. My next sale walked in the door - it was a business exec looking to lose weight. As we got into the sales presentation, she told me the program wouldn't work for her because she went out to eat for lunch everyday. Normally, I would have lost this sale. I was a stickler for making people *not* eat out. But I really *needed* the money. Refusing to lose the sale because of this *one thing*, I conceded "I'll make you an eating out guide for when you go to restaurants so you can eat out 100 percent of the time and still hit your goal. How does that sound?" She agreed, and I closed the sale.

I took the time to make an eating out guide for her. But from that point going forward, whenever someone said "but what about eating out??" I had the solution. Over time, I continued solving obstacles with templates and trainings until there were no more "*one things*" to prevent my sales. This lesson has stuck with me to this day. Don't get romantic about *how* you want to solve the problem. Find a way to solve every problem a prospect presents with. When you do that, you make an offer that's so good, people just can't say no. And that's what we're building here.

Note: You must resolve every obstacle a buyer believes they will have to convert the highest amount of people. That's not to say that if you don't, you won't sell people. Not at all. But you won't sell *as many people as you otherwise could have*. And that's the goal, to sell the most people, for the highest possible price, with the highest possible margin.

Step #5: Trim & Stack

Now that we have enumerated our potential solutions, we will have a gigantic list. Next, I look at the cost of providing these solutions to me (the business). I remove the ones that are high cost and low value first. Then I remove low cost, low value items.

If you aren't sure what's high value, go through the value equation and ask yourself which of these things will this person:

1) Financially value

2) Cause them to believe they will be likely to succeed

3) Make them feel like they can do it with much less effort and sacrifice

4) Help them accomplish their goal and see the result they want with far less time investment.

What should remain are offer items that are 1) low cost, high value and 2) high cost, high value.

Example: Let's say I moved in with someone and did their shopping, exercising, and cooking for them. They would probably believe they would definitely lose weight. But I am not willing to do that for any amount of money short of a gazillion dollars.

The next question becomes, is there a lesser version of this experience that I can deliver at scale?

Just take one step back at a time until you arrive at something that has a time commitment or cost you are willing to live with (or, obviously, massively increase your price so it becomes worth it for you — i.e., the gazillion dollars to live with someone).

If there's *one* type of delivery vehicle to focus on, it's creating high value, "one to many" solutions. These will be the ones that typically have the biggest discrepancy between cost and value. For example, before I started my first gym, I had an online training business. I created a small excel sheet application that after inputting all of someone's goals, automatically generated over 100 meals perfectly suited to their macronutrient and calorie needs. Better yet, depending which meals they selected, would tell them what they needed to buy at the grocery store in exact amounts, *and* how to prepare them in bulk for their exact amounts. It took me about 100 hours to put the whole thing together. But from that point going forward I sold truly personalized eating plans for very expensive prices, but they only took me about 15minutes to make. High value. Low cost.

These types of solutions require a high, one-time cost of creation, but infinitely low additional effort after. (Fyi - This is exactly why software becomes so valuable).

That doesn't mean you don't ever want to do something in a small group or one-on-one model. After all, I do 1-on-1 with all of my portfolio company CEOs that we help scale past $30m+. You just want to make sure you save those high cost items for *big* value adds only. If you think you can accomplish the same value with a lower cost alternative, then do that instead.

When I was running my gym, I went through this exercise and created: bulking blueprints, an eating-out system, a travel eating and workout guide, meal plans for every bodyweight and gender, a grocery list calculator, plateau busting meal plans (for when they got stuck), fast cooking guides partnered with meal prep services, and did in-person nutrition orientations with every client one-on-one.

Many of the "one to many" solutions require more up front work. Once created, however, they become valuable assets that create value in perpetuity. It's worth putting in the time to create these because they will create high margin profit for years to come.

Real talk: the meal plans I made for my gym have been used by 4,000+ gyms now and literally hundreds of thousands of people. They are simple and easy to follow. So they have provided ample return for the week or two of dedicated time I spent making them.

And if you ever have the desire to build a repeatable business model, something that scales, these assets you create will become the bedrock. This book, for example, is a high-value asset that is low cost overall. Sure, it costs me a lot up front, but each additional book I sell after my first one costs me very little and provides tremendous value.

The Final High Value Deliverable

Let's sum this up before we configure our final high value deliverable.

Step #1: We figured out our prospective client's dream outcome.

Step #2: We listed out all the obstacles they're likely to encounter on their way (our opportunities for value).

Step #3: We listed all those obstacles as solutions.

Step #4: We figured out all the different ways we could deliver those solutions.

Step #5a: We trimmed those ways down to only the things that were the highest value and lowest cost to us.

All we have to do now is…

Step #5b: Put all the bundles together into the ultimate high value deliverable.

So let's go back to the example. We see our prospects struggled with the following:

Format Note

I'm going to display each problem-solution set as:

Problem → Solution Wording→ Sexier Name for Bundle .

Then, underneath, you will see the actual delivery vehicle (what we're actually gonna do for them/provide)

Buying food→ How anyone can buy food fast, easy, cheaply → Foolproof Bargain Grocery System . . . that'll save hundreds of dollars per month on your food and take less time than your current shopping routine ($1,000 value for the money it'll save you from this point on in your life)

    a. 1-on-1 Nutrition Orientation where I explain how to use…

    b. Recoded grocery tour

    c. DIY Grocery Calculator

    d. Each plan comes with it's own list for each week

    e. Bargain grocery shopping training

    f. Grocery Buddy System

    g. Pre-made insta-cart grocery carts for delivery

    h. And a check-in via text weekly.

Cooking→ Ready in 5min Busy Parent Cooking Guide . . . how anyone can eat healthy even if they have no time ($600 value from getting 200 hours per year back — that's four weeks of work!)

a) 1-on-1 Nutrition Orientation where I explain how to use…

b) Meal Prep Instructions

c) DIY Meal Prep Calculator

d) Each plan comes with it's own meal prep instructions for each week

e) Meal prep buddy system

f) Healthy snacks in under 5min guide

g) A weekly post they make to tag me for feedback

Eating→ Personalized Lick Your Fingers Good Meal Plan . . . so good it'll be easier to follow than eating what you used to "cheat" with and cost less! ($500 value)

a) 1-on-1 Nutrition Orientation where I explain how to use…

b) Personalized Meal Plan

c) 5min Morning shake guide

d) 5min Budget Lunches

e) 5min Budget Dinners

f) Family size meals

g) A daily picture of their meals

h) 1-on-1 feedback meeting to make adjustments to their plan (and upsell them)

Exercise→ Fat Burning Workouts Proven To Burn More Fat Than Doing It Alone . . . adjusted to your needs so you never go too fast, plateau, or risk injury ($699 value)

Traveling→ The Ultimate Tone Up While You Travel Eating & Workout Blueprint . . . for getting amazing workouts in with no equipment so you don't feel guilty enjoying yourself ($199 value)

How to actually stick with it→ The "Never Fall Off" Accountability System . . . the unbeatable system that works without your permission (it's even gotten people who hate coming to the gym to look forward to showing up) ($1000 value)

How To Be Social→ The 'Live It Up While Slimming Down" Eating Out System that will give you the freedom to eat out and live life without feeling like the "odd man out" ($349 value)

Total value: $4,351 (!) All for only $599.

Author Note

Most of our facilities now sell this bundle for longer periods of time for $2,400 to $5,200. *Wild.* As we got better at creating and monetizing value, the prices and profit of our facilities skyrocketed. Once you start down this value creation process, each additional piece of value you create stacks on top over time. This is why it is important to begin.

Can you see how much more valuable this is than a gym membership? The bundle does three core things:

1) Solves *all* the perceived problems (not just some)

2) Gives you the conviction that what you're selling is one of a kind (very important)

3) Makes it impossible to compare or confuse your business or offering with the one down the street

Whew! We finally have what we are going to deliver in all its glory. That being said, it is unlikely we would present it in this way. Depending on whether we sell one on one or one to many, we would present this differently. I will address how to present each of these bundled items in the bonus section (next section).

Summary Points

We went through this entire process to accomplish one objective: to create a valuable offer that is differentiated and unable to be compared to anything else in the marketplace. We are selling something unique. As such, we are no longer bound by the normal pricing forces of commoditization. Prospects will now only make a *value-based* rather than a *price-based* decision on whether they should buy from us. Hoorah!

Now that we have our core offer, the next section will be dedicated to *enhancing* it. We will employ a combination of psychological levers: bonuses, urgency, scarcity, guarantees, and naming.

> **Free Gift #6: BONUS Tutorial: Offer Creation Part II:**
>
> If you want to walk through the profit maximizing trimming & stacking process with me live, go to Acquisition.com/training/offers and select "Creating Offers Part 2". You'll also find some checklists I made to make this process more streamlined for you so you can reuse for each product you make. As always, it's absolutely free. Enjoy.

SECTION IV
Enhancing Your Offer

Scarcity, Urgency, Bonuses, Guarantees, and Naming

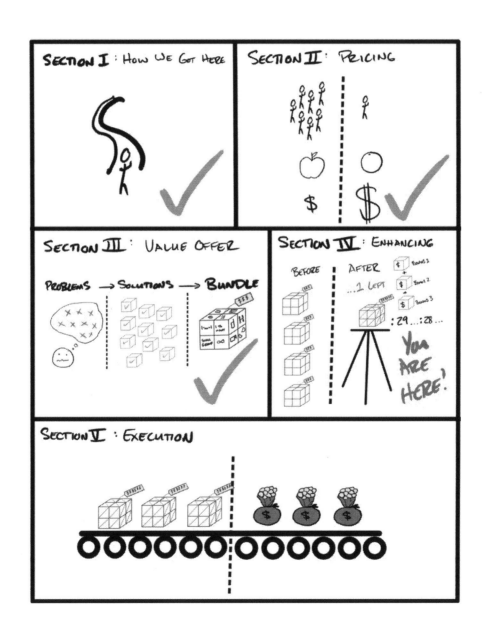

Enhancing The Offer: Scarcity, Urgency, Bonuses, Guarantees, and Naming

"But wait . . . there's more, if you order today . . . "

- Every infomercial in the 90s

May 2019. Arnold Scwarzenegger's home. After School All Stars Fundraiser.

The line of cars outside Arnold's house was around the corner . . . and we were in one of them. We were sitting in our Uber when a security guard with an earpiece, black suit, and black sunglasses knocked on the driver's window. It was like straight out of a movie.

The driver rolled down the window. "Name?"

"Alex and Leila Hormozi."

He scanned the list on his clipboard, nodded, then checked off our names. "Great," he said. His demeanor transformed from stern to inviting. "Welcome to the fundraiser. Stay in this line. You'll make a left, then security will escort you the rest of the way."

The security guard talked into his walkie talkie to the next post down the road, signaling our car was approved.

Pulling up to the front of the estate was like entering into a Bond movie. Lamborghinis, Bugattis, Ferraris, and brands of cars that are too expensive to even speak of. Old guys with young, scantily-clad girls. A-List Actors. Celebrities with millions of followers who were recording themselves as they arrived, talking through their iphones to their audiences. And us.

The fundraiser was $25,000 per ticket to attend, with an invite list of only 100. There was a red carpet and all. Every year, the fundraiser culminated in a big auction for memorabilia and items some of the business owners in the audience gave away for charity.

We walked around looking at the entertainment stations purposely devised to get donors in the "giving mood." We saw $10,000 scotches . . . $500 cigars . . . pre-released items from major brands that wouldn't be available to the public until months later. And, of course, the most expensive cuisine you could imagine. Leila and I were just soaking it all in. It was a wonderful night. We definitely felt like cool kids.

Ben, the CEO of the charity, saw us looking lost and walked over. He took me by the arm to introduce me to some of the other donors. These were all men who were older than me and donating $100,000 and up without a second thought.

The man he introduced me to was one of the charity's biggest donors. He had built an ultra-high end jewelry and watch business. I'm talking $100,000, $500,000, $2,000,000+ rare status symbols that people buy only so other .001 percenters know they belong. He had donated upwards of $700,000 in merchandise as prizes for the fundraiser that evening.

"Alex and Leila, meet George," Ben said. "He's been very generous with his time and money to the cause. George, this is Alex and Leila Hormozi. They're donating $1,000,000 tonight to ASAS. I figured you are both good people and wanted to connect you two."

"Nice to meet you both," George said with calm, weathered eyes. He was in his late sixties, tall and sturdily built. You could hear his eastern block origins in his accent. He sounded like a man who had fought tooth and nail to be here, but had softened his demeanor for gatherings such as these. But the tiger with teeth and claws remained under the surface, ready to be called upon at a moment's notice. I felt like I understood this guy.

Ben broke the ice. "So....George was the one who got me to raise the price from $15,000 per ticket to $25,000. We had more demand than ever this year. But I took his advice. I cut the amount of tickets we sold *and* raised the prices."

"That's right," said George, content that his sage business advice had been followed. "When demand increases, cut supply." He perked up slightly as we talked about money.

This man had built his business from nothing and had found ways to sell things for extraordinary profits by understanding human psychology. I had long learned about supply and demand, but this guy was using its psychological underpinnings to fuel a fundraising. You could take the tiger out of the jungle, but not the jungle out of the tiger.

People want what they can't have. People want what other people want. People want things only a select few have access to. He was dead right. They had raised an *extra* one million dollars that night before the event had even started by cutting the supply of tickets *and* raising the prices. On top of that, all the people were more qualified than ever to be big donors. The night ended up being the most successful night in the charity's history, raising nearly $5,400,000 from only 100 people (that's $54,000 per head!). Each of the items was auctioned off as a one-of-a-kind item. And if you missed it, you would never have a chance again to buy it. Arnold even threw in some bonuses when two people would get high enough in the bidding, allowing the charity to get both donations.

It was a masterful display of human psychology at work in a setting where people were knowingly over-paying for products. *The products remained unchanged*, yet within this setting, an item that wouldn't sell at a different venue for $10,000 sold for $100,000. That's how powerful scarcity, urgency, and bonuses are. And breaking down how to use them to further increase demand for your offer, without changing your offer, is the purpose of this section.

Author Note - Other Persuasion Powers At Play

Scarcity, urgency, bonuses, and guarantees were not the *only* persuasion tools being employed to get egregious prices at the fundraiser. They also used commitment and consistency, status, peer pressure, goodwill, celebrity endorsements, competition, etc. However, scarcity, urgency, and bonuses are the only three I will be breaking down in this book as I believe they belong more with the "offer" and less with the actual "selling," which I will talk about in depth in Acquisition: Volume IV $100M Sales.

The Delicate Dance of Desire

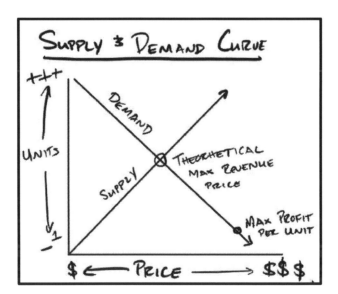

Fundamentally, all marketing exists to influence the supply and demand curve. We artificially increase the demand for our products and services through some sort of persuasive communication. When we increase the demand, we can sell more units. When we decrease supply, we can sell those units for more money. The "perfect profit combination" is lots of demand, and very little supply, or *perceived* supply. The process of enhancing your core offer is designed to do both of these things: increase demand and decrease *perceived* supply so that you can sell the *same* products for *more* money than you otherwise could, and in *higher* volumes than you otherwise would (over a longer time horizon).

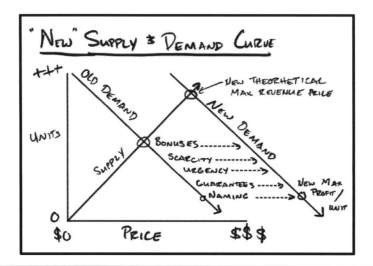

Author Note:

This assumes a regular business who is not trying to gain mass market penetration for some other strategic advantage.

Desire comes from *not* getting what you want. In fact, I heard this quote that I love from Naval Ravikant: "Desire is a contract you make with yourself to be unhappy until you get what you want." It follows, therefore, that we only want things we do *not* have. As soon as we have them, our desire for them disappears. Therefore, if we seek to increase the demand (or desire), we must decrease or *delay* satisfying the desires of our prospects. We must sell *fewer* units than we otherwise *can*. Let that sit with you for a second.

Consider this example. We promote some two-day workshop that is upcoming. First we whisper that it's coming. Then we tease it with some of the benefits. Then we shout that it is launching in a week. Then, when we launch this amazing workshop. We have two supply-demand scenarios:

Scenario one: We sell 10 units at $500 each (sell entire pyramid at price all say yes)

Scenario two: We sell two one-day workshops 1-on-1 for $5000 each. (skim top of pyramid, with 80 percent not purchasing)

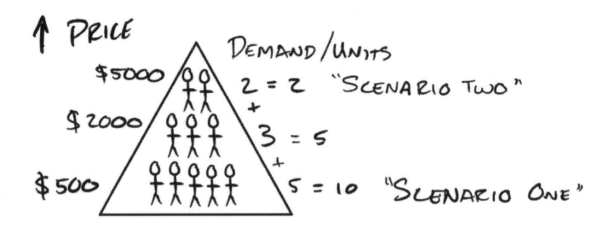

It's worth noting that each of these prospects have a different buying threshold. In my experience, demand for services is non-linear. Instead, I've found demand to be fractal (80/20). In other words, one fifth of the prospects are willing to pay five times the price (or more).

In the example, I might have ten people willing to pay $500, but two of them willing to pay $5000. So, I would make more, have lower costs (more profits), provide more value, and increase the demand in the remaining prospect base by selling *fewer* units. Think about how exclusive scenario one vs scenario two would *feel*. Think about all the people who would want to purchase, but would not be able to. Would this increase or decrease their desire? It would increase it, of course.

On top of that, if people see that others who 'were able to get in' are loving it, it would further increase their desire. And the next time, they would act with more urgency, and be willing to pay *more* for the same thing than they originally did. So now, in the aftermath of our second scenario, we still have eight people who have unsatisfied desire. This increases their desire further. And to boot, we now have new prospects who weren't in the original pool who now want what we have.

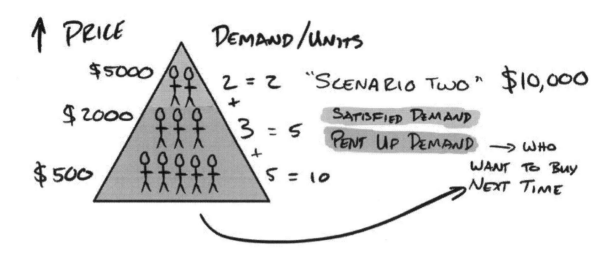

The next time we promote scenario two, we then open *three* spots at the same price and sell them all (still leaving some prospects with pent up demand!). This is a continuous theme.

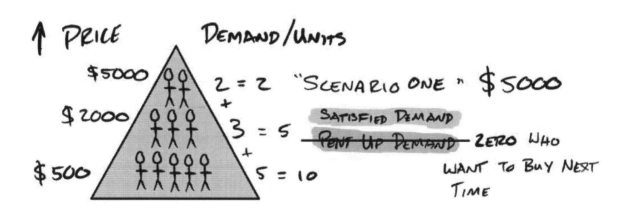

Conversely, if we were to promote scenario one again (the $500 price point), we would probably sell fewer slots the second time around. Why? We have no pent up demand. All desire has been satisfied. When you "pull the trigger too early," each successive instance we promote, we sell even fewer. Eventually, we run out of sufficient demand to make even a single sale. This is the sad state many businesses find themselves in *always trying to generate more demand* to make another quick sale.

Hormozi Law: The longer you delay the ask, the bigger the ask you can make. "The longer the runway, the bigger the plane that can take off."

We must endeavor to keep our supply (and satisfaction of desire) under the demand that we are able to generate. This maximizes profits and keeps desire ravenous in our customer base. This is the real key to never going hungry.

Summary Points

The reason I titled this sub-section "Delicate Dance of Desire" is that supply and demand are inversely correlated (in theory). If you satisfy zero desire (provide zero supply), you will not make money, and *eventually* leave people feeling rejected (Note: it takes much longer than you think).

Conversely, if you satisfy all the demand, you will kill your golden goose, and not know where your next meal will come from. Mastering supply and demand comes from the elegant dance between the two. If you sleep with your significant other everyday they have less desire than if you haven't slept with them for a week. We want the ravenous prospect, not merely the aroused.

Therefore, understanding the interplay between these variables is key to enhancing your offer and the amount of profits you will make *over time*. Up to this point, we have covered all the things *inside* of your offer that can make it immune to price comparison and transform regular services and products into things that people *will find a way to pay for*. It would follow that the next variable that can make your offer more desirable is how it is presented. In other words, the *outside* variables that position the product in your prospect's mind. These forces are often more powerful than your core offer. In this next section Enhancing Your Offer, I will show you how I:

1) Use *scarcity* to decrease supply to raise prices (and indirectly increase demand through perceived exclusiveness)

2) Use *urgency* to increase demand by decreasing the action threshold of a prospect.

3) Use *bonuses* to increase demand (and increase *perceived exclusivity*).

4) Use *guarantees* to increase demand by reversing risk.

5) Use *names* to re-stimulate demand and expand awareness of my offer to my target audience.

I will define each, then give you examples of how to use them. We will use all these variables to enhance our offer and shift the demand curve in our favor, leaving our customers always wanting for more. We will start by tactically stimulating "fear of missing out" aka *FOMO* through *scarcity*.

Enhancing The Offer: Scarcity

"Sold out."

SCARCITY (X LEFT / Y SPOTS) ⤷ # OF UNITS/AVAILABILITY   SOLD OUT !

Scarcity is one of the most powerful and least understood forces to unlock unlimited pricing power. If you want to learn how to sell air for millions of dollars, then pay attention.

The reason an authority (like a doctor), a celebrity (like Oprah), or a celebrity authority (like Dr.Oz or Dr.Phil) can charge egregious rates is because of *implied* demand. People assume that there is a lot of demand for their time, and, therefore, not a big supply of it. As a result, it must be expensive.

That being said, it's hard for most businesses to understand what it's really like to have an uneven supply-demand curve until you've experienced it. I'm going to try and walk you through what it felt like for me the first time I experienced it in order to give you a taste of the power.

When I got into this world of acquisition, I saw mentors of mine selling days of time for $50,000+. My mind was blown for two reasons. First, because I didn't understand how they could make so much money for a single day. Second, because I didn't understand who in their right mind was buying it. Over time, I learned.

I'll start with the buyer. If I have a rare problem, and I *must* solve this problem for my own pursuit of happiness, it will consume all of my attention. By the nature of my problem being specialized, there will be very few people who can solve it. This means there is not a large supply of solvers. In many cases, I will perceive only one possible "solver" (Supply = 1).

Beyond that, if solving this problem speeds up my achievement of a goal by a year or two, or immediately results in me making hundreds of thousands of dollars, or millions of dollars, that solution becomes far more valuable, does it not? Of course it does. And so, it would follow, if I can pay someone $50,000 for a day of their time, and see an increase of $500,000 per month in revenue within three months because of the insights and strategies revealed, that would be a helluva return on investment, right?

So there are two components to the value: first, how rare the sources are; second, the actual value being provided. The value and rarity compound to create some truly breathtaking profits.

Specialized consultants are paid millions of dollars to solve problems worth tens of millions to clients. The client pays for all the experience and expertise the expert has and avoids the cost of errors (time and money). In short, they skip the bad stuff and go straight to the good stuff more quickly and for less money than it would cost to figure it out on their own . . . a beautiful economic exchange.

I personally experienced this for the first time when I had two *different* people offer me $50,000 for a day of my time after speaking at an event. They were scaling an education business in a niche (not too dissimilar from my own) and could not get past the $1M per month mark. As someone who was doing $1M per *week* in the same business type (at the time), I was a *very* specific type of person with the keys to their problem.

So what happened, you ask? *Drum roll . . .* I didn't accept their offers. Why? Because I was making more than $50,000 per day in profit from my business and didn't want the distraction.

After the event concluded and I was speaking with Leila, I realized how I had somehow become 'one of those people I had always wondered about'. It was a very surreal experience for me. I finally understood how premium prices were *truly* made . . . simple supply and demand. There is little that substitutes for incredible demand. You can try and fake it, but there is a special type of "0 fucks given" vibe that's hard to replicate when you truly do not need a person's money (or even want it).

That's how these guys can charge so much . . . because they don't need it. The person who needs the exchange less always has the upper hand. I always try to remember that. It's one of the negotiating and pricing principles that has best served me in my life.

"But Alex, how are you going to show me how to use scarcity to increase the amount of people who want my offer when currently no one does?" Great question. Let's attack some real-world, in-the-trenches strategies to *reliably* create scarcity .

Creating Scarcity

When there's a fixed supply or quantity of products or services that are available for purchase it creates "scarcity" or a "fear of missing out." It increases the need to take action, and by extension, purchase your offer. This is where you publicly share that you are only giving away X amount of products or can only handle Y new clients.

For example, if a musician drops a limited edition hoodie and says he only made 100 and they will never be made again, are you more or less likely to buy it than one that is always available? More likely, naturally. The idea that you can *never* get it again makes it more desirable.

This is an example of scarcity. It is the fear of missing out on something. It pulls on our psychological fear of loss to get us to take action. Humans are far more motivated to take action to hoard a scarce resource than they are to act on something that could *help* them. *Fear of loss* is stronger than *desire for gain*. We will wield this psychological lever to get your clients to buy in a frenzy, all at once, until you are *sold out*.

Three Types of Scarcity

1) Limited Supply of Seats/Slots: in general or over X period of time.

2) Limited Supply of Bonuses

3) Never available again.

But how do you use this properly without being phony? I'll try and give you some real world examples

<u>Physical Products</u>

Having limited releases is a tried and true method of using this psychological bias to your advantage. You can have limited releases for flavors, colors, designs, sizes, etc. "This month, we are releasing 100 boxes of mint chocolate cookie flavored protein bars." Important point: to properly utilize this method you <u>should *always* sell out.</u>

Here's why: it's better to sell out consistently than over order and fail at creating that scarcity. This method stacks in effectiveness if it is done repeatedly over time (just not too often). Once a month seems to be the sweet spot for most of the companies that I know who do this with regularity.

Second Important Note: When using this tactic, you must also let everyone know that you sold out. That is part of what makes it work so well. This way, even people who were on the fence, when they see that it was sold out, it gives social proof that *other people* thought it was worth it. And now that the choice has been made for them, they desire it more because there is no way they can get it. So the next time you make the offer they will be far more likely to take you up on it.

Fun fact: Chanel, a brand that has maintained insane margins and pricing for over a century, is a master of scarcity. They send only 1-2 of each piece to each store so every store has a different selection and every item is the last or second to last item in stock. This allows them to price far above market and turn buying impulses into purchases.

Services

With services, especially if you want to consistently get customers, it can be a little trickier to use scarcity. But I will show you a few simple ways to employ scarcity ethically to increase your take rates on offers. These all have similar elements with very slight tweaks. I'm enumerating these because one of these might mentally fit your business model more than others.

1) **Total Business Cap - Only accepting....X Clients.** Only accepting X clients at this level of service (on-going). This puts a cap on how many clients you service but also keeps them in it. You create a waiting list for new prospects. The moment the door opens, they jump right in and price resistance disappears. Periodically, you can increase capacity by 10-20% then cap it again. This works well for your highest tiers or service levels.

   a) This is like saying "My agency only will service twenty-five customers total. Period." Over time you can increase your prices and squeeze the lower performing accounts out and bring in new more profitable accounts, or, you can periodically 'open slots' as your capacity allows (always leaving some demand unmet).

2) **Growth Rate Cap - Only accepting X clients _per week_ (on-going)** "We only accept 5 new clients per week and we already have the first 3 spots taken. I have 6 more calls this week, so you can take the spot or one of my next calls and you can wait until we reopen." I have used this method since the beginning of my business. I always knew what my capacity was per week, and simply chose to let our prospects know how many openings we had left. This banks on the fact that you can only handle a certain amount of new clients anyways, on a regular basis, so you might as well let them know it.

3) **Cohort Cap - Only accepting....X clients _per class or cohort_.** Similar to the above, except done on whatever cadence you desire. Only accepting X amount per class or cohort over a given period is another way of thinking about it. Imagine you only start clients monthly or quarterly. This helps you get some cadences in place in your business operationally while also allowing your sales team some legitimate scarcity. Example: "We take on 100 clients 4 times a year. We open the doors then close them." Etc.

Let me give you a real example of scarcity to enhance the value of a free lead magnet. If I were to tell you right now that I have a checklist that you can download for free that has all these materials for you in this book in bulleted format, you *might* be inclined to put this book down and go there to download it now.

But, if I told you I have it set so that every week the page only allows *twenty* new people to download it, you'd be far _more likely_ to go see if you can grab it. And even more so if when you try it, you see that it has already run out for the week. Result? You join a list that notifies you the next time twenty more checklists become available for download. What happens next? When you get that notification, you'll hit the link on your phone and go to the page because you don't want to miss out again.

By employing scarcity, we make what would otherwise be a "neat free download" into a desirable thing not everyone has access to. You also, by extension, would be far more likely to consume it when you do get your hands on it . . . all because of how we controlled supply. Cool, right?

Honest Scarcity (The Most Ethical Scarcity)

The easiest scarcity strategy is <u>honesty</u>. Wait, what? Let me explain.

I'm sure right now, you probably couldn't handle 1,000 clients tomorrow right? But how many could you handle? 5? 10? 25? Well, you might as well define a number that you are willing to take on in a given time period, then advertise that. Simply letting people know that you are three-fourths of the way to capacity this week will move people over the edge to buying from you. Or letting people know that you are 81% to capacity in your total business, will make people more likely to sign up with you "before they lose the chance." Scarcity also implies within it, social proof. If you are 81% to capacity then a decent amount of people made the decision to work with you, and the closer you get to your arbitrary fullness, the faster the spots will disappear. But only you get to draw where that line is "full." Neat right?

Summary Points

Employ one or multiple methods of scarcity in your business. You will drive a faster purchasing decision from your prospects, and at higher prices. Just let them know your limits and let psychology do the rest.

Now that we've covered some of my favorite scarcity tactics that you can use year round, what else could you do to increase demand *without* changing anything about your offer? Increase urgency. We will cover that next.

Pro Tip - Extreme Scarcity

If you don't hate money, sell a *very* limited supply of 1-on-1 access. You can do that via any of the mediums described in "Delivery Cube." Direct message access. Email Access. Phone access. Voice memo access. Zoom access. Etc. There are lots of ways you can do this. But I promise you this - if you want to immediately make a lot of money, create a *very* exclusive service level based on access to you (yes, unscalable), that you cap at a *tiny* number. Price it *very* high. Then, tell people. You will make more money than you thought possible. These also tend to be some of the best clients. And limit your delivery to something that you don't hate. For me, I hate emails and messages but dont mind zoom calls. Make it work for your working style. The cream of the crop (the 1% of 1% will adjust and take action).

Pro Tip - Once You're Out, You Can Never Come Back

You can create scarcity by also capping your service level *and* saying that if they leave than can never return. This type of scarcity makes people think extra hard about leaving. I started doing this with my gyms early on. Then I was in a mastermind that employed this. Then I started using it in my higher level of Gym Lords. This works best with small groups (like the above example). As groups become much bigger, the tactic loses some teeth (speaking from experience).

Enhancing The Offer: Urgency

"Deadlines. Drive. Decisions."

- Me

URGENCY (BY X DATE)
→ RELATES TO TIME

5...4...3...2...1...DONE!

Scarcity is a function of *quantity*. Urgency is a function of *time*.

This is where you *only* limit *when* people can sign up, rather than *how many*. Having a defined deadline or cut off for a purchase or action to occur creates urgency. Frequently, scarcity and urgency are used together, but I will separate them out for you to illustrate the concepts.

I'm going to show you my four favorite ways of using urgency on a consistent basis, ethically: 1) Rolling Cohorts, 2) Rolling Seasonal Urgency, and 3) Promotional or Pricing Urgency 4) Exploding Opportunity. They will employ urgency in your business without being phony. My favorite way of doing this is having cohorts of clients start on a regular cadence. This has the added operational benefit of helping you create a choreographed onboarding experience for new clients. As you scale, this will become increasingly important.

1) Cohort-Based Rolling Urgency

For example, if you start clients every week (even in unlimited amounts), you can say: *"If you sign up today, I can get you in with our next group that kicks off on Monday, otherwise you'll have to wait until our next kickoff date."*

If you wanted to juice it up a little bit, you could say: *"I actually had a client who signed up a few weeks ago drop out, so I have an opening for our next cohort that kicks off on Monday. If you are pretty sure you're gonna do this sooner or later, might as well get in on it now so you can start reaping the rewards sooner rather than paying the same and waiting."*

Those two tweaks above have pushed so many sales over the edge by just reminding a potential customer that if they sign up, they will be starting on Monday, and if they do not, they will have to wait a week. It's small things like this that nudge people to take the action they know they should take anyways.

Obviously the less frequently you kick off new customers, the more powerful this is. For example, if you only start clients two times a year, people will be very inclined to sign up, especially as the date approaches. Even starting new clients every other week can confer this urgency nudge.

What if I lose sales by turning business away?

Just like guarantees, there is always a fear that you will make less money by employing this strategy. We are afraid that we will lose sales we would have otherwise made. Every experienced marketer on the planet will tell you - it is a fear, and it is unfounded. The biggest sales on a week long campaign or launch happen in the last 4 hours of the last day (up to 50-60%). That means that the last 3% of the time allotted creates 50-60% of the sales…that's completely illogical, but also unmistakably *human*. So, just like a guarantee, you will make more money from the many people who decided to take action than people who actually missed out because in reality, those people were never going to buy (heck, they didn't even buy when they had their fee to the fire, so why would they without?) Good to remember.

What to do if you just started a cohort and someone wants to buy….

You have two options: 1) you can offer them a speedy personalized onboarding to get them up to speed as a "bonus" for signing up today and still get them in. Or, my preference, 2) You can explain to them that since the next group starts in a little, they will have the advantage of having more time to review the materials, talk to their employees (for b2b products) or family members (for b2c products). On top of that, they can have a more extended payment plan that you can only make available to them since the start date is so far out . . . an advantage that most clients do not get. In the end, remember, you always have the advantage because you are the one who calls the shots.

2) Rolling Seasonal Urgency

In a digital setting, having actual sign up date countdowns is *very* useful. But make sure they are real. If they aren't, you'll lose credibility and just look *like every other wannabe marketer*. This is very common with internet businesses that use "launch" models. I personally *love* having the dates that I am running a promotion through on my landing pages *and* in my copy. I want it to be visible everywhere. The nice thing is that you can always fire up another ad campaign and a new landing page with new dates and be right as rain. You will see your conversions go through the roof, and it takes maybe five minutes of editing — well worth the time investment.

Example: Our New Year Promotion ends Jan 30!

Next Month: Our Valentines Lovers Promo Ends Feb 30!

Next Month: Our Sexy By Spring Special Ends March 31!

Next Month: Our Fools in Love April Promo Ends April 30!

The actual promotion may be the same, but naming it something different "by season" gives you a "real" differentiator that gives you a start and a finish. Deadlines drive decisions. By simply having these, you can point to them and let human beings push themselves over the edge so as not to miss out.

> **Pro Tip - Local Businesses:** This is my number one strategy for local businesses. They must vary their marketing more frequently than national advertisers. Putting a new wrapper with a date on the same core service gives you urgency and novelty that will consistently outperform the "same old" campaigns.

3) Pricing or Bonus-Based Urgency

This is another way of creating urgency using your actual offer or promotion/pricing structure as the thing they could miss out on (kind of brilliant!). It allows businesses that sell clients year round to still use urgency. For example, *"Yes, let's get you started today so you can take advantage of the discount you came in for. I'm not sure how long we will be running it as we change them every 4 weeks or so, and this is one of the better ones we have run in a while."*

This creates some fear of missing out on the promotion (or discount or bonuses), rather than your actual service. It would be a lie to say that if you own a roofing business you won't service them if they buy after the date. But, if you talk specifically about the promotion you can often elicit the same urgency on buying in the prospect while maintaining your integrity — win-win. You can interchange a pricing promotion, discount, or added bonuses like free install or free onboarding or an extra workshop (valued at $1,000) if they buy now. These are all things you can swap around your core offer to create urgency.

Pro Tip - Clean Your Pipeline With Every Price Change: If you ever really are planning on raising your prices (hopefully soon if you are reading this book!) then you can always clean out your pipeline by letting people know "The price is going up! So get in now!" Never raise your prices without letting people know. It shows a position of strength *and* will give you a nice little influx of cash from the people in the pipeline who were on the fence.

---

4) Exploding Opportunity

On occasion you will be exposing the prospect to an arbitrage opportunity. The opportunity itself has a ticking time clock, as all great opportunities do. Every second someone delays, they miss out on disproportionate gains.

Example: If I was explaining an arbitrage opportunity between buying products on ebay and selling them on amazon, this market inefficiency would over time correct itself. The sooner someone acts the better it will be for them. This could be true for selling someone on the opportunity of trading crypto currencies, buying a stock, getting into a new platform to advertise before competitors jump on the bandwagon. Highly competitive job environments often get job offers that are "exploding offers" everyday they wait to take the job, their pay or bonuses decrease. This forces prospects to make fast decisions rather than try and "wait it out" to see if they get a better offer.

All of these examples show opportunities that decay with time, so if you find yourself in front of an opportunity like this, make sure to emphasize it!

Summary Points

Adding a deadline and incorporating one or multiple forms of urgency will get more people to take action than would otherwise. I have employed all four of these methods with great effectiveness. I suggest you do the same. Next up….Bonuses!

Free Gift #7: Bonus Tutorial: How to Ethically Use Scarcity & Urgency

If you want to walk through some live (ethical) examples of scarcity & urgency with me, go to **Acquisition.com/training/offers** and select **"Scarcity & Urgency"** to watch a short video tutorial. You'll also be able to grab my **Scarcity & Urgency Checklist** I use when creating offers. As always, it's absolutely free. Enjoy.

Enhancing The Offer: Bonuses

"It's all gravy baby"

- Play on an old English saying.

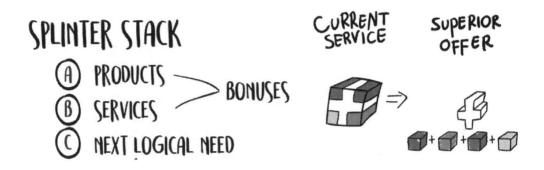

I have to give special thanks to Jason Fladlien for my renewed appreciation for bonuses. They are so powerful that they earned an entire chapter. In this chapter, I'm going to cover: what to offer, how to pick them, how to value them, how to present them, how to price them.

The main point I want you to take away from this is that *a single offer is less valuable than the same offer broken into its component parts and stacked as bonuses (see image).* The entirety of our offer we came up with at the end of the last section. This section is about how to present those pieces in what order. For example, I may in fact do lots of things in my service, but until I enumerate them, they are unknown. This is why every infomercial of all time continues on with "but wait....there's more!"

They would not use these techniques unless they were effective, as every second of air time costs money and must be justified with ROI. You'll also notice that if you watch those old infomercials, they would sell one knife for $38.95 then include 37 other knives, sharpeners, pans, and guarantees to beat the prospect into submission. They establish the price, then they expand upon it until you feel *it's such a good deal it would be stupid to pass it up.*

The reason this works is we are increasing the prospect's price-to-value discrepancy by increasing the value delivered instead of cutting the price. We anchor the price we tell them to the core offer. Then with each increasingly valuable bonus, that discrepancy grows wider and wider until it's too big to bear and we snap the rubber band in their mind that is holding their wallet in their pocket.

We are now going to present that "stack" of deliverables that we assembled earlier in a way that makes them irresistible.

Pro Tip: Add Bonuses Instead of Discounting Whenever Possible on Core Offers

Whenever trying to close a deal, never discount the main offer. It teaches your customers that your prices are negotiable (which is terrible). Adding bonuses to increase value to close the deal is far superior to cutting prices. It puts you in a position of strength and goodwill rather than weakness.

Presenting Bonuses 1-on-1 vs Group Selling

There are key differences between pitching to a group versus a single person. Group selling is beyond the scope of this book. But I want to at least address when a bonus would be brought up in a 1-1 selling scenario. When selling one on one, you ask for the sale *first,* before offering the bonuses. If they say yes, then after they have signed up, you let them know the *additional* bonuses they're going to get. This creates a *wow experience* and reinforces their decision to buy.

On the other hand, if the person does *not* buy after the first ask, then you present a bonus that matches their perceived obstacle, then ask again. Don't feel weird about asking again. You simply agree with the prospect, add the bonus, and ask if this consolation was "Fair enough." People have a hard time rejecting reciprocity, so adding a bonus to accommodate, then another, then another, and people will feel almost obligated to buy from you.

If you recall from our "Trim and Stack" chapter, each of those deliverables is now being weaponized and presented at the perfect time. We're going to provide all these bonuses to them anyways, but it increases the perception of our offer's value by layering these bonuses one at a time.

Bonus Bullets

That being said, there are a few key things to remember when offering bonuses:

1) Always offer them (you can use the bulleted bundle we came up with at the end of Section III)

2) Give them a special name that has a benefit in the title

3) Tell them:

   a) How it relates to their issue

   b) What it is

   c) How you discovered it, or what you had to do to create it

   d) How it will specifically improve their lives or make their experience

      i) Faster, easier or less effort/sacrifice (value equation)

4) Provide some proof (this can be a stat, a past client, or personal experience) to prove that this thing is valuable

5) Paint a vivid mental image of what their life will be like *assuming* they have already used it and are experiencing the benefits

6) Always ascribe a price tag to them and justify it

7) Tools & checklists are better than additional trainings (as the effort & time are lower with the former, so the value is higher. The value equation still reigns supreme).

8) They should each address a specific concern/obstacle in the prospects mind about why they can't or won't be successful (bonus should prove their belief incorrect)

9) This can also be what they would logically realize they will need next. You want to solve their next problem before they even encounter it.

10) The value of the bonuses should eclipse the value of the core offer. Psychologically as you continue to add offers, it continues to expand the price to value discrepancy. It also, subconsciously communicates that the core offer *must* be valuable because if these are the bonuses, the main thing has to be more valuable than the bonuses right? (No, but you can use this psychological bias to make your offer seem wildly compelling).

11) You can further enhance the value of your bonuses by adding scarcity and urgency to the bonus themselves (which takes this technique and puts it on steroids).

    a) <u>Bonuses With Scarcity</u>

        <u>Version 1</u>: Only people who sign up for XZY program will have access to my Bonus #1, 2, 3 that are never for sale or available anywhere else other than through this program.

        <u>Version 2</u>: I have 3 tickets left to my $5,000 virtual event, if you buy this program you can get one of the last 3 tickets as a bonus.

    b) <u>Bonuses With Urgency</u>

        <u>Version 1</u>: If you buy today, I will add in XYZ bonus that normally costs $1,000, for free. And I'll do that because I want to reward action takers.

    c) With hope, you can see the subtle differences. The first two examples aren't constrained by time. They state that if you buy the program you will get things you normally would not be able to. The bonus with urgency is about them buying *today*, and if they do not buy today, they lose those bonuses. Minor difference, but worth noting.

Advanced Level Bonuses - Other People's Products and Services

You can get other businesses to give you their services and products as a part of your bonuses in exchange for exposure to your clients for free. This is free marketing for them, and high value products for you at no cost. Businesses will do this because you are going to give their business exposure for free to the highest quality prospects, your customers. As long as they are not direct competitors, you can get some brownie points, secure some future referral IOUs, and make your offer more valuable at the same time. If you secure enough of these relationships, you can literally justify your entire price in the savings and additional true-to-price bonuses.

For example - if I owned a pain clinic, I might get a massage therapist to give me 1-2 free massages to incorporate into my offer. On top of that, I might get:

...a chiropractor to give me two free adjustments. (Value: $100)

...a low inflammation food company to give me discounts for their products ($50 savings)

...discounts for braces and orthotics ($150 savings)

...a local health club down the street to give me a personal training session for free and a free month of membership to their pool ($100 Value)

...discounts on pharmaceutical drugs from the local pharmacist ($100/mo in savings)

...repeat the above for multiple service providers (so perhaps I get ten chiropractors to all give me a free adjustment, now I have ten free adjustments in my bundle.

...Etc

Now if my offer was $400, then the value of these free bonuses ALONE is worth more than the $400.

As if that weren't already awesome enough, if you really want to be a jedi, negotiate a group discount *and* a commission to yourself. This is exactly what we did with our supplement company. Our gym owner clients who use our sister supplement company Prestige Labs sponsored athletes get a 30% discount on our products, on top of that, the sponsored athlete gets paid 40% of all sales netted after the applied discount.

So it's a win-win for everyone. Their clients get it for 30% less than our main site. They get paid for giving away exclusive discounts. And we get customers in exchange for the commission paid. Everyone wins.

If you are following along, each of these bonuses can become revenue streams for you indirectly by getting clients to say YES more easily, and directly because you can negotiate that each of these businesses can pay you for the people you send their way.

So let's also say we negotiated the following "affiliate commissions" for making the introduction to these businesses.

...the chiro gives you $100 per person who comes into their office

...the food company gives you free food (yum!)

...orthotics company gives you $100 per person referred

...health club gives you a free membership OR $50 per person who signs up

...pharmacy gives you $100 per person

Now let's look at how much money we made...our $400 offer now has the possibility of making us an extra $350...*pure profit*! That's the beauty of these relationships. The other businesses will pay you and you don't have to do *anything* but refer customers to them that you have already spent the money to acquire.

And if you *really* want to get crazy, come up with a grand slam offer with these partner businesses by using the same concepts in the book so that each of the bonuses themselves becomes even more valuable than a simple commoditized service.

Free Gift #8: BONUS...on...BONUSES

There are a million and one ways to use bonuses in your offers. You can get people to act faster. You can price anchor and product anchor (little known). You can get more people to say yes than you otherwise would. If you want to a live deep dive with me on this, go to **Acquisition.com/training/offers** and select **"Bonus Creation"** to watch a short video tutorial. I also have a **Free Bonus Checklist** I use when creating offers. Swipe it for your own business on the house!

Summary

We want to employ bonuses because they expand the price to value discrepancy and get people to purchase who otherwise wouldn't. They massively increase the prospects' perception of the value of our offer. So here's what to do:

1) Create checklists, tools, swipe files, scripts, templates, and anything else that would take lots of time and effort to create on one's own, but is easy to use once created. Anything that you can invest in one time that clearly cost time or money to create, but can be given away endless time is a perfect fit for a bonus.

2) Beyond that, make a habit to record every workshop, every webinar, every event, every interview and use them as additional bonuses (as needed to crush a perceived obstacle).

3) Proactively negotiate group discounts and a referral commission with adjacent businesses that solve needs your customer will have as a result of beginning this process with you. What's the next natural thing they might want? Go to those businesses, get a deal for them they could never get for themselves (because you are negotiating with the purchasing power of all your customers at once, very powerful).

Author Note: The longer you are in business the more of these bonus assets you will have at your disposal. All of these things are valuable. Put them in a vault and keep them in your back pocket to sprinkle into an offer to get the deal closed. Information products work very well here because they have high perceived value, low cost, and zero operational effort besides giving an additional login. Tickets to virtual experiences or events work too. Same goes for a higher level of service that has a fixed cost like giving someone VIP service for a month (which also doubles as a way of upselling them into that level of service to keep them on it . . . more on that in Book II.)

What should be a bonus vs part of the core offer if I am the one fulfilling it?

Short answer: Wow Factor - in other words - something you wouldn't want someone to miss. Many times you have so much "stuff" you will be providing your customers (good thing) that valuable nuggets can get lost in the mix. You want to take the most distinct ones that can almost stand on their own and pull those out to highlight them. This is especially true for things that are short in length but high in quality or value. Checklists or infographics can condense a lot of information into a small space. Someone might not feel justified paying lots of money for a product launch map (for example) but as a bonus would be perceived as very valuable.

Next Up . . .

We have our core offer. We are presenting it in a way to increase scarcity and urgency to increase the likelihood they want it even more. We stacked the bonuses of our offer to make the price to value discrepancy out of this world and break our prospects' minds. Next on our magical journey will be addressing the big elephant in the room...*risk*. We will completely obliterate it using a combination of guarantees so they have no reason not to buy.

Enhancing The Offer: Guarantees

"You're gonna like the way you look...I guarantee it."

- Men's Warehouse ad that ran forever.

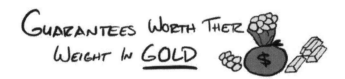

The single greatest objection for any product or service being sold is...drum roll...*risk*. Risk that it doesn't do what it's supposed to do for them. Therefore, reversing risk is an immediate way to make any offer more attractive. You will want to spend a disproportionate amount of time figuring out how you want to reverse it. That being said, how much more attractive can a guarantee make an offer?

Jason Fladlien, who I referenced earlier, once stated that he had seen the conversion on an offer 2-4x simply by changing the quality of the guarantee. It's that important.

From an overarching perspective there are four types of guarantees: 1) Unconditional 2) Conditional 3) Anti-Guarantee 4) Implied Guarantees. You must *always* hit your guarantee hard, even if you don't have one. Say it boldly and give the reason why.

But won't people take advantage of a crazy guarantee?

Sometimes, but not usually. That being said, you must understand the math. If you close 130 percent as many people, and your refund percentage *doubles* from 5 percent to 10 percent, you've still made 1.23x the money, or 23 percent more, and that all goes to the bottom line.

Ex: 100 sales, 5 refunds (5%) = 95 Net Sales

Guarantee Offer 130 sales, 13 refunds (10%)= 117 Net sales

117/95 = 1.23x (23% increase)

Don't be emotional, just do the math. For a guarantee to *not* be worth it, the increase in sales would have to be 100 percent offset by people who refunded. So an absolute increase in sales of 5 percent would need to be offset by an absolute increase in refunds of 5 percent (but that might be a doubling of refunds, which is unlikely). So, for the most part, the stronger the guarantee, the higher the *net* increase in total purchases, even if the refund rate increases alongside it.

<u>Warning</u>: While guarantees can be effective sellers, people who buy *because* of guarantees can become very shitty customers. A person who only buys because of a guarantee is a person who may not be willing to put in the work necessary to see success with your product or service. In a world where you want to reverse risk *and* get customers the best outcome possible, tying your guarantee to the things they need to do to be successful can help all parties.

Pro Tip: High Cost Services Warning

If you have a tremendous amount of cost associated with your product or service, you will likely want to employ a conditional guarantee or an ANTI guarantee, as you will have to eat the cost of the refund AND the cost of fulfilling.

Types of Guarantees

"IF You Dont Achieve X in Y Time We Will...

What makes a guarantee have power is a conditional statement: If you do not get X result in Y time period, we will Z.

To give a guarantee *teeth* you have to decide what you'll do if they *don't* get the result. Without the "or what" portion of the guarantee, it sounds weak and diluted.

Note: This is what most marketers do.

Bad Example: We will get you 20 clients guaranteed.

Better example: You will get 20 clients in your first 30 days, or we give you your money back + your advertising dollars spent with us. This is a simple, but strong guarantee.

Here are the four types of guarantees. I'll go over them in theory then we will apply them.

1) Unconditional Guarantees

As I stated earlier, there are unconditional, conditional, and "anti-" guarantees. Unconditional are the strongest guarantees. They're basically a trial where they pay first then see if they like it. This gets a LOT more people to buy, but you *will* have some people refund, especially as consumer culture continues to shift towards entitlement and zero accountability.

2) Conditional Guarantees

Conditional guarantees include "terms and conditions" to the guarantee. These are the ones you can get VERY creative on. In general, you want these to be "better than money back" guarantees. Because if they are going to make an investment, you want to match their investment psychologically with an equal or higher perceived commitment. These also can have a *very* powerful effect on getting clients results. If you know the key actions someone must take in order to be successful, make those part of the conditional guarantee. In a perfect world, 100% of your customers would qualify for a conditional guarantee, but will have achieved their result, and therefore will not want to take it. That is an ideal we can all aspire towards. And just fyi - if given the option of getting a refund or getting the outcome they were promised the vast majority of people will take the outcome.

3) Anti-Guarantees

Anti-guarantees are when you explicitly state "all sales are final." You will want to own this position. You must come up with a creative "reason why" the sales are final. Typically, you'll want to show a massive exposure or vulnerability on your part that a consumer could immediately understand and think "Yes, that makes sense." These types of guarantees are especially important with items that are consumable or massively diminish in value once given.

4) Implied Guarantees

Implied guarantees are any offer that is a performance-based offer. This comes in many different forms. Revshare, profitshare, triggers, ratchets, monetary bonuses, etc are all examples. The end all concept is the same, if I don't perform, I don't get paid. Unique to this particular structure, it also confers the upside of "If I do a great job, I will be very well compensated." These only work in situations where you have transparency for measuring the outcome and trust (or control) that you will get compensated when you do perform.

Stacking Guarantees

An experienced salesman understands that, like bonuses, you can actually *stack* guarantees. For example, you could give an unconditional 30 day no questions asked guarantee then on top of that give a conditional triple your money back 90 day guarantee. That would be an example of stacking an unconditional with a conditional guarantee.

You can also stack two conditional guarantees around different (or sequential) outcomes. For example, you'll make $10,000 by 60 days, $30,000 by 90 days as long as you do thing 1, 2, and 3. This future paces the prospect into an outcome they now believe is far more likely (since you will be deliberately spelling it out in a conditional guarantee with a timeline for achievement). Doing this shows the prospect you are serious about getting them results and convinced that they will achieve what they want. This shifts the burden of risk back from them onto us...a very powerful strategy.

Let's go through some different guarantee examples:

Guarantee: If you don't achieve X, in Y time, we will [insert offer] . . .

[Unconditional] "No Questions Asked" Refund Guarantee

What the Client Gets: A) a full refund, B) a 50 percent refund, C) a refund of their ad spend and any ancillary costs incurred, D) you pay for a competitors program instead, E) you return their money plus an additional $1,000 (or other applicable amount)

My Take: This is about as simple as it gets. It's also very risky. You put yourself in a situation where if someone does not achieve the results, whether because of your fault or not, you will still be held accountable. Obviously this is a strong, but unoriginal guarantee. You can add conditions, but the more conditions you add, the faster this guarantee loses its teeth.

Wording: I heard Jason Fladlien, who I referenced earlier, pitch his unconditional guarantee on a webinar and I thought it was unbelievable. These are 100% his words and not my own. I take no credit for this but have included it for completeness.

"I'm not asking you to decide yes or no today...I'm asking you to make a fully informed decision, that is all. The only way you can make a fully informed decision is on the inside, not the outside. So you get on the inside and see if everything we say on this webinar is true and valuable to you. Then, if it is, that's when you decide to keep it. If it's not for you, no hard feelings. You will then, after signing up at URL be able to make a fully informed decision that this isn't for you. But you can't make this decision right now for the same reason you don't buy a house without first looking at the inside of it. And know this...whether it's 29 min or 29 days from now...if you ain't happy, I ain't happy. For any reason whatsoever, if you want your money back you can get it because I only want to keep your money if you're happy. All you have to do is go to support@xyz.com and tell use "gimme my money" and you got it, and in short order - our response times to any support request average 61 min over a 24/7 time period. You can only make such a guarantee when you're confident that what you have is the real deal and I'm fairly confident that when you sign up at URL you're getting exactly what you need to BENEFIT."

Pro Tip: Name Your Guarantee Something Cool

If you are going to give a guarantee, spice it up. Instead of using "satisfaction" or some other "vanilla" word, describe it more strongly.

Generic Example (Bad): 30 Day Money Back Satisfaction Guarantee.

Creative Imagery Example #1 (Good): In 30 days, if you wouldn't jump into shark infested waters to get our product back, we will return every dollar you paid.

Creative Imagery Example #2 (Great): You'll get our famous "Club a Baby Seal Guarantee"After 30 days of using our services, if you wouldn't club a baby seal to stay on as a customer, you don't have to pay a penny.

[Unconditional] Satisfaction-Based Refund Guarantee (Expanded from above):

What the Client Gets: If at any time they're not satisfied with the level of service they're receiving from you, they can request a refund (at any time) for the program.

My Take: Believe it or not, this was my guarantee when I sold weight-loss programs. Besides being an irresistible offer, I guaranteed satisfaction. I used the strength of my guarantee to close a lot of deals. "Do you think I'd still be in business if I gave a crazy guarantee like that and wasn't good at what I did? Now I'm *not* guaranteeing you're going to hit this goal in six weeks, after all, because I can't eat the food for you. But I am guaranteeing that you will get $500 worth of value and service from us to support you. If you don't feel like we gave you that level of service, I'll write you a check the day you tell me we suck."

It works perfectly with a best-case/worst-case close. "Best case you get the body of your dreams and we give you all your money towards staying with us to hit your long-term goal. Worst case you tell me I suck, I write you a check, and you get six weeks of free training. Both options are risk free. But, the only thing guaranteed *not* to help you is walking out of here today." If you are good at what you do, you can use a guarantee like this to push a lot of people over the edge. That line made me a lot of money. I had two people take me up on it out of 4,000 sales in three and a half years.

Satisfaction/No questions asked is the highest form of guarantee. It means we could do everything right and you could still ask for your money back. As long as you know the math, you will typically make up for the refunds in spaces with higher and faster closing on the sales side. *But you have to be good at fulfilling your promises.* If not, steer clear. I believe this offer works much better in lower-ticket situations. It becomes very risky as you go into higher-ticket services with higher costs of fulfillment.

Pro Tip: Unconditional vs Conditional Based on Business Type

Bigger broader guarantees work better with lower ticket B2C businesses (many people just won't bother taking the time). The higher the ticket, and the more business oriented it is, the more you want to steer towards specific guarantees. That may or may not include refunds, and may or may not have conditions.

[Conditional] Outsized Refund Guarantee

What the Client Gets: Double or Triple their money back, or a no-strings-attached payment of $X,XXX (or another amount that's far more than what they paid).

My Take: This is for when you sell something with high margins. And this is a guarantee to add *with* a consumption condition. That means they must do a variety of things to qualify for this guarantee. A world class affiliate marketer Jason Fladlien (who did $27M in a single day) recently used an amazing guarantee for a course he sold. He said "if you buy this course and spend $X on advertising your ecommerce store using the methods herein, and don't make money, I will buy your store from you for $25,000 no questions asked." He claimed that an additional $3M in sales came from this crazy guarantee on a $2997 course. What's more, he only gave 10 of these $25,000 refunds out. So the refund generated $2.75M in extra sales. That's what a crazy guarantee does for you.

In general, a very strong guarantee like this will definitely drive more sales. This really serves the purpose when you need a *lot* of stuff to be done by your prospect, and, assuming those things are done, there's a low chance of the result not being achieved. Sometimes a guarantee like this can actually get clients better results on top. This guarantee will typically outperform a traditional 30-day money back guarantee in terms of net conversions (sales minus refunds).

[Conditional] Service Guarantee

What the Client Gets: You keep working for them free of charge until X is achieved.

My Take: This is probably my personal favorite guarantee of all time. It essentially guarantees they will achieve their goal, but it eliminates the element of time. You are never at risk for losing the money. The guarantee is around the outcome. To add further flavor to it, you can make this guarantee conditional on them doing key actions linked with success: setting up a web page, attending calls, showing up to workouts, weighing in, reporting data, etc.

Real Talk: Since I have been advising businesses to use this particular guarantee, I have yet to have a single person say a client took them up on it. Realistically, if someone actually does everything you asked them to do and doesn't achieve the result by the time you had said, one of two things usually happens:

1) Seeing your client's commitment, you happily keep working with them until they achieve the desired result

2) It gets dropped. Your client is likely very close to the goal, which means satisfied. Also, it's likely the sales conversation with the guarantee was months earlier. What may have been important in the sales conversation is a distant memory now, replaced by their affection towards you/your business.

[Conditional] Modified Service Guarantee

What the Client Gets: You give them another Y-long period of service or access to your product/services free of charge. Generally, Y should give them at least twice the duration.

My Take: This is like the service guarantee, but it ties a specific duration to your extended work/involvement. So instead of being on the hook "forever," you're only on the hook for an additional Y period of time. I've seen it work magically and keep the business on the hook for a more finite period of time which may be an easier place for you to start before doing the "all out" Service Guarantee above.

[Conditional] Credit-based Guarantee

What the Client Gets: You give them back what they paid but in a credit toward any service you offer.

My Take: This is best used during an upsell process to seal the deal on a service they are unsure they will like. They already like what they have, you are trying to sell them *more* of that. Worst case, they can apply it to the thing they already like. So it maintains goodwill with the customer.

[Conditional] Personal Service Guarantee

What the Client Gets: You work with them one-on-one, free of charge, until they reach X objective or result.

My Take: This is absolutely one of the strongest guarantees in existence. It's like a service guarantee on crack. You will *definitely* want to add conditions, though: they must respond back in twenty-four hours, they must use the products you tell them to, they must XYZ. Only if they do that, will you keep working with them one-on-one.

This is especially powerful as you scale and become more edified as a business owner. Can you imagine one of my sales people saying, "Alex will personally work with you until your offer converts"? Right. It would work. It would also be a nightmare. So I would probably put contingencies like, "Provided you've already spent $10,000 on your existing offer using our structure, the offer you ran was for lead generation, and it was a free offer. These are things that would make it unlikely they would not succeed. If for some reason they *hadn't* with those stipulations in place, I could probably fix their problem in ten minutes just looking at it.

[Conditional] Hotel + Airfare Perks Guarantee

What the Client Gets: If you don't receive value, we will reimburse your product *and your* hotel + airfare.

My Take: This is technically a "refund of ancillary costs" from our first example. I just love it a lot for workshops and in-person experiences. Normally the event would cost more than the hotel and airfare, so it's like adding an extra $1000 to a guarantee but way more tangible. It's original enough that people like it.

[Conditional] Wage-Payment Guarantee

What the Client Gets: You offer to pay their hourly rate, whatever that may be, if they don't find your call/session with them valuable.

My Take: This is also an ancillary cost guarantee, just a very original one. If someone ever actually asks for the wage payment, just ask them for their tax return and divide it by 1,960 (number of working hours at 40hrs/wk for a year). But no one asking for a refund will actually do that, so you will never actually have to give one of these out. Like ever.

[Conditional] Release of Service Guarantee

What the Client Gets: You let them out of their contract free of charge.

My Take: This voids a commitment or cancellation fee. If you have a business that has enforceable commitments, contracts or clauses, this can be a powerful guarantee. Better yet, if you are in a business that does not enforce your contracts, then you have nothing to lose by adding the guarantee.

[Conditional] Delayed Second Payment Guarantee

What the Client Gets: You won't bill them again until *after* they make or get their first outcome. Ex: Lose your first five pounds . . . make your first sale . . . get your website live, etc.

My Take: I like this a lot, especially if you have a very systematized process for getting the first result. It gets the prospect thinking in fast action terms and gets them moving. It will also focus your team on activating your client. This is a great one when you know what metric or action drives activation (predicting indicator of long term retention) of a client. I've successfully used this guarantee loads of times.

[Conditional] First Outcome Guarantee

What the Client Gets: You continue to pay their ancillary costs (ad spend, hotel, etc) until they reach their first outcome. Example: If you don't make your first sale in 14 days, we will pay for your ad spend until you do.

My Take: Just like the delayed second payment, just centered around a different cost. I personally like this setup a lot. It keeps everyone focused on getting that first dollar over the bridge. Once that one comes across, the second comes soon after.

[Anti-Guarantee] All Sales Are Final

What the Client Gets: Access to super exclusive very valuable service/product. Likely, this is a very powerful thing that once seen cannot be unseen, or once used cannot be taken away. Example: a line of code to improve your checkout experience on a website. Once someone received this code, they could try and use it without paying you. Or a series of opening messages for picking up girls, or opening sentences for messaging cold prospects. Things that are very valuable but incredibly easy to steal after they've been seen/understood.

My Take: This can enhance the persuasiveness of the sale and the value of the product or service. It essentially *implies* that the client is going to use it and see an immense benefit thereby exposing the business to vulnerability. It acts as a damaging admission. We have an "all sales are final" policy, *but* that is because our product is so exclusive and so powerful that once used it cannot be unused." Since it is so standard to have some sort of guarantee, not having one is attention-worthy.

So instead of being wishy-washy, lean into the fact this thing works so well, and is so easy to copy, you *must* make all sales final. They'll believe you even more if you take this position. "We are going to show you our proprietary process that we are using right now to generate leads in our business. Our funnels, ads, and metrics. We're going to be exposing the inner workings of our business, as a result, all sales are final." Note: strong reason why is needed here. Just make one up that sounds compelling. The more you can show *real* exposure, the more effective this will be.

Anti-guarantees can also work very well with high ticket products and services that require a lot of work or customization. "If you're the type of customer who needs a guarantee before taking a jump, then you are not the type of person we want to work with. We want motivated self-starters who can follow instructions and are not looking for a way out before they even begin. If you are not serious, don't buy it. But if you are, boy are you going to make a killing. " From these examples, you should get the idea.

Implied Guarantees: Performance Models, Revshares, and Profit-Sharing

Performance: A) …Only pay me \$XXX per sale/ \$XXX per show B) \$XX per Lb Lost

Revshare: A) 10% of top line revenue B) 20% profit share C) 25% of revenue growth from baseline

Profit-Share: A) X% of profit B) X% of Gross Profit

Ratchets: 10% if over X, 20% if over Y, 30% if over Z

Bonuses/Triggers: I get X when Y occurs.

What The Client Gets: If you do not perform, they do not have to pay. If you perform, your compensation has been determined based on an agreement decided upon *before* you begin working.

My Take: Performance, Revshare, and Profit-shares aren't guarantees "per se", but for all intents and purposes, they are. There is an implied guarantee whenever you enter into a revshare or performance partnership: if you dont make money, you don't have to pay me. In my opinion, this is one of, if not THE most desirable setup. First because it makes you accountable to your clients' results. Second it weeds out low performers. Perfect alignment between client and service provider fosters collaboration and a long-term relationship. I'm a big fan. The drawbacks are tracking and collection. So if you can find a way around that…you've hit a gold mine. This is a part of the offer we teach our agencies who use our software. We help them switch from a retainer model to a performance model and wrap that into the Grand Slam Offer I walked through earlier. I've seen countless agencies go from \$20k/mo to \$200k+/mo in a matter of a few months.

You can also pair a revshare or performance setup with a minimum. It would be like saying "we get the greater of \$1000 or 10% of revenue generated." So if the client doesn't generate money because of whatever reason this at least covers your costs of services etc.

Or saying we get $1000/mo for the first 3 months, then after that, it switches to 100% performance. This would be ideal for a setup that takes a lot of time to get going.

These types of offers work well when you have quantifiable outcomes. The stronger, of course, is no guaranteed payment without performance.

Create Your Own Winning Guarantee

Reversing risk is the number one way to increase the conversion of an offer. Experienced marketers spend as much time crafting their guarantees as the deliverables themselves. It's that important.

I have personally used all the guarantees listed above (except for the hotel and phone call one, which I just saw and liked). But you can come up with your own! The key is to identify a client's biggest fears, pain, and perceived obstacles. "What do they *not* want to have happen if they pay you? What are they most afraid of?" Reverse their fears into a guarantee. Think of the time, emotion, and outside costs associated with any program or service. The more specific and creative the guarantee is, the better.

That being said, guarantees are enhancers. They can enhance the magnetism or attraction of any offer, but they cannot make a business. If a guarantee is used to cover up a poor sales team or a poor product, it will backfire into lots of refunds. No bueno.

My advice: Start selling service-based guarantees or setting up performance partnerships. This will make all sales final (so no fear from refunds). Most importantly, it will commit you to your customers' results and keep you honest. From there, either keep that guarantee and scale (perfectly fine), or move up the food chain to less restrictive guarantees to increase volume.

We now have a core offer built and guarantees chosen.

Next Up...

Now all we have to do is put a bow on this puppy and actually name it. Naming an offer correctly determines how well your advertising converts, how big of a response you get from outbound emails/cold calls/texts, and how many inbound responses you get from organic comments.

It matters.

That being said, I will show you how to generate unlimited names or "wrapping paper" for your offer. That way it never fatigues, no matter how small your market may be. This is the key to evergreen lead generation.

Free Gift # 9 BONUS: Create A Winning Guarantee With Me

Guarantees can make or break businesses. They are like dynamite, they can be incredibly powerful *if* in the hands of an expert. Go to **Acquisition.com/training/offers** and select **"Creating Guarantees"** to watch a short video tutorial so you can start using this in your business to make more sales ASAP. I also made a **Free Guarantee Checklist** for you to use when thinking through all the variables. As always, it's absolutely free. Enjoy.

Enhancing The Offer: Naming

Implicit-egotism effect: we are generally drawn to the things and people that most resemble us.

M-A-G-I-C HEADLINE FORMULA

Like the tree that falls in the forest that no one hears, having a Grand Slam Offer will not make you money if no one finds out about it. The goal must be that upon hearing about your offer, your ideal prospects are interested enough to take action. Naming it properly is an integral part of this process.

Here's an example. Say you see a "Free Six-Week Stress Release Challenge" and a "Float Tank Center Session." While they may be the same thing, just named differently, you're much more likely to respond to the first.

Now here's the rub: over time, offers fatigue. And in local markets, they fatigue even faster. Why? In a local market, it costs relatively little to reach an entire population. On most platforms you can reach 1,000 people for about $20. So, if there are 200,000 people in your addressable area, then it would only cost you $10,000 to reach all of them one time.

Important disclaimer: reaching an audience one time in *no way* means an offer is fatigued. Most people don't even notice an offer on the first mention. That's why you need to create new creative (videos, images) and new hooks, stories, and copy around the same offers. You can still use offers for a long time. But when we're talking about *years* of use, not months, offers can eventually fatigue.

Over time you can rename the offer to refresh it. This one concept will get you leads forever. I mean it. So pay attention. We are *not* changing the actual offer. We are only changing the *wrapping paper*.

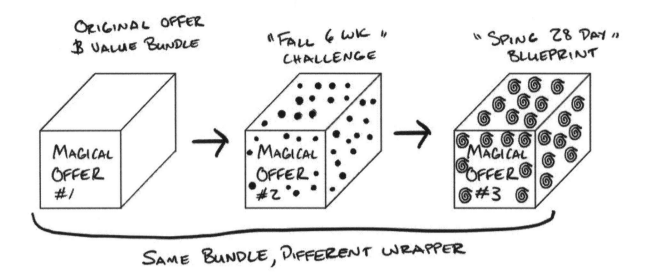

ORIGINAL OFFER
$ VALUE BUNDLE

"FALL 6 WK" CHALLENGE

"SPING 28 DAY" BLUEPRINT

MAGICAL OFFER #1

MAGICAL OFFER #2

MAGICAL OFFER #3

SAME BUNDLE, DIFFERENT WRAPPER

If you've put together a bundled offering, you're still ultimately going to be doing the same things. The work you do, services you provide, and products you offer will remain unchanged as the name shifts. Again, we're simply changing the wrapper.

Here's the simplest formula I've come up with for this process:

M-A-G-I-C HEADLINE FORMULA

MAGNET — **M**AKE A MAGNETIC REASON

AVATAR — **A**NNOUNCE THE AVATAR

GOAL → **G**IVE THEM A GOAL

INTERVAL — **I**NDICATE A TIME INTERVAL

CONTAINER — **C**OMPLETE WITH A CONTAINER WORD

Important Note: Not all these components are mandatory. You will typically use three to five of them in naming a program or service. If you can fit them all in, great, but it's likely the name will become too long.

The shorter and punchier the better. So it's a balance between brevity and specificity. The only way to really know what works is to write the names out and test them.

Let's run through the components now.

Author Note: Marketing Theory

If you like understanding the concepts behind my chosen M-A-G-I-C formula. Each roughly translates to: Attention (M-Magnet), Discrimination (A-Avatar), Purpose (G-Goal), Timeline (I-Interval), and Method (C-Container).

Make a Magnetic "Reason Why"

We start the name with a word or phrase that tells people the "reason why" we are running our promotion.

I like to tell people to think like a fraternity party planner. When I was in college, we had a party once because a guy got his wisdom teeth removed. I say this to say. . .the "reason why" can literally be anything.

It really doesn't matter so long as you believe it. And you can even make a joke of it like the fraternity example. But this should answer one or both of the following questions: *Why are they making this great offer?* or *Why should I respond to this offer?/What's in it for me?*

Examples: Free, 88% off, Giveaway; 88% off, Spring, Summer, Back To School; Grand Opening; New Management; New Building; Anniversary; Halloween; New Year.

Note: I will discuss how to monetize free and discounted offers in Volume III: Money Models.

Announce Your Avatar

This component calls out your ideal avatar: who you are looking for and who you are not looking for as a client. You want to be as specific as possible, but no more. When in a local area, the more local you can make your headline, the more it will convert. So don't do a city, try and go to the sub market, or hyper local area. Not Baltimore but Towson, MD. Not Chicago, but Hinsdale, Etc.

Examples: Bee Cave Dentists, Rolling Hills Moms, Brick & Mortar Businesses, Salon Owners, Retired Athletes, Brooklyn Busy Executives

Give Them A Goal

This is where you articulate your prospect's dream outcome. It can be a single word or a phrase. It can be an event, a feeling, an experience, or an outcome, anything that would excite them. The more specific and tangible, the better.

Examples: Pain Free, Celebrity Smile, 1st Place, Never Out Of Breath, Perfect Product, Grand Slam Offer, Little Black Dress, Double Your Profit, First Client, High Ticket, 7 Figure, 100k, Etc.

Indicate a Time Interval

You're just letting people know the duration to expect here. This gives an example of how long your results will take to achieve.

Note: If you're making any sort of quantifiable claim (like income gain or weight loss) most platforms will *not* approve this type of messaging *with* a stated duration to achievement because it implies a guarantee. It implies they are going to get this outcome in a period of time, which goes against many platform rules. So dont give a quantifiable outcome with the duration unless your platform allows it. That being said, duration is a powerful component of a Grand Slam Offer and you should definitely use it anywhere you don't need to deal with compliance. Alternatively, if the goal you help them with is not a "claim" per se, then absolutely use a time interval. "$10,000 in 10 days" vs "Make Your First Sale in 10 Days."

Examples: AA Minutes, BB Hours, CC Days, DD Weeks, Z Months. "4 Hour" "21 Day" "6 Week" "3 Month"

Complete With A Container Word

The container word denotes that this offer is a bundle of lots of things put together. It's a system. It's something that can't be held up to a commoditized alternative.

Examples: Challenge, Blueprint, Bootcamp, Intensive, Incubator, Masterclass, Program, Detox, Experience, Summit, Accelerator, Fast Track, Shortcut, Sprint, Launch, Slingshot, Catapult, Explosion, System, Getaway, Meetup, Transformation, Mastermind, Launch, Game Plan, Deep Dive, Workshop, Comeback, Rebirth, Attack, Assault, Reset, Solution, Hack, Cheatcode, Liftoff, Etc.

Pro Tip: Find Time To Rhyme

Good rhymes stick in people's minds. Rhyme your program name to win the game.

Google "rhyming dictionary" for an easy shortcut. Note - Don't try and force it. It's not a requirement, it's just a "nice-to-have".

Ex: Six-Pack Fast Track, 5-Day Book Print Sprint, Marriage Thrive Deep Dive, 12-Week 2-Putt Shortcut, 12-Month No-Debt Reset, Celebrity Butt Shortcut, Get Some Ass Masterclass (just thought it was funny), etc. You get the idea.

> **Pro Tip: Alliteration**
>
> Alliteration is when you make all (or most) of the words start with the same letter or sound.
>
> An alternative approach to rhyming is to use alliteration when naming your program. This is easier for most people than rhyming. Again, you do not need to rhyme or alliterate. Don't force it.
>
> **Ex:** Make Money Masterclass, Change Your Life Challenge, Big Booty Bootcamp, Debt Detox, Real Estate Reset, Life Coach Liftoff, Etc.

I might be weird, but naming offers is one of my favorite parts of this process. What I want to highlight, yet again, is that your actual money model, pricing, and services will remain largely unchanged. Changing the wrapper simply means changing the exterior perception of what your Grand Slam Offer is.

Below you'll find a few examples of named offers for different industries.

Wellness

Free Six-Week Lean-By-Halloween Challenge

88% Off 12-Week Bikini Blueprint

Free 21-Day Mommy Makeover

60-minute Make Your Friends Jealous Model Hair System

Six-Week Stress-Release Challenge

(Free!) Bend Over Pain Free in 42 Days . . . Healing Fast Track

Doctors

$2,000-Off Celebrity Smile Transformation

Lakeway Moms - $1,500 Off Your Kids Braces

Lakeway Moms - 12 Months To A Perfect Smile ($1000 off for 15 families)

Back to School Free Braces Giveaway

Grand Opening Free X-Ray & Treatment - Instant Relief

Back Sore No More! 90 Day Rapid Healing Intensive (81% off!)

Tightness? $1 Massage New Client Summer Special

Coaching

5 Clients in 5 Days Blueprint

7F Agency 12 Week Intensive

14 Day Find Your Perfect Product Launch

Fill Your Gym in 30 Days (Free!)

I could keep listing these, but hopefully you get the idea. Now it's time for you to give it a try for your Grand Slam Offer.

Again, you don't necessarily have to use all the power components of the headline. Using three to five will typically create something that is more unique and desirable, allowing you to separate yourself from the competitive field and create an offer that will get clicks and engagement, and ultimately make you money.

Furthermore, you don't need to do them in the M-A-G-I-C order. Do what sounds punchier to you. After doing this for a while, you'll see that some offers convert better than others. That's natural. And every once in a while you'll get a name that takes off like a rocket. I honestly have no idea why some names win and others do not. So, don't be emotional about it. Keep trying. Keep striking out. Then try more. You'll get there.

Now that you have several working names for your offer, you can use two to three of your best names in your advertising campaign. Quickly note the winner, then use that as a control to test against with new names. That is how you promote.

What Happens When Offers Fatigue

As you market offers, you will need to create variations over time as the tastes of the market change over time. Here's the order in which you will change things to keep lead flow consistent.

1) Change the creative (the images and pictures in your ads)

2) Change the body copy in your ads

3) Change the headline - the "wrapper" of your offer

    a) Free 6 Week Lean Challenge to Free 6 Week Tone Challenge

    b) Holiday Hangover to New Year New You

4) Change the duration of your offer

5) Change the enhancer of your offer (your free/discount component)

6) Change the monetization structure, the series of offers you give prospects, and the price points associated with them (Book II)

I follow this variation framework because most of the time it's the first handful of items that need to be changed. Typically, they need to be changed again and again without touching anything on the bottom of the list.

For example, when ads fatigue, we don't change our entire business; we just run the same ad again with a different video or image. Once that stops working, we change it again. Eventually you need to change the words in your ads. And repeat the process. Then, and only then, would you change the wrapper.

Let's say we change from a Six-Week Stress Release Challenge to a 42-Day Relaxing Holidays Challenge for a massage center. Same core offer, just a different wrapper. Then, of course, you could change the duration of your offer - six weeks to 28 days or eight weeks, etc. The lower on the list you go, the more operationally heavy it is, so really be sure you have exhausted the earlier "lighter" ways of varying your offer.

Once you've monetized an offer, rarely should you change it. Just rinse and repeat over and over and over again. This can be hard because we are entrepreneurs and *love* change. Change here usually just creates inefficiency and operational drag, costing you money. No bueno.

So use your entrepreneurial ADD on the "wrapper" first - the "look and feel" of the offer (copy, creative, headlines). Then change the seasonality of the offer. Then change the duration. If you're still stuck, change what you are giving away for free or discount. Change the entire machine behind it *only* as a last resort and for a darn good reason, especially once you get traction.

But how do you get initial traction? Good question. Try the offer structure and headline that you think has the highest likelihood of working. Then stick with it.

And if they don't convert at first, don't worry. You'll get better. Oftentimes, if you are using these types of models, *many* of them will work. In that case, stick with the one that gives you the highest return. You can also rotate between offers if it doesn't create lots of operational drag for your type of business. This is the ultimate position of power. You have multiple "aces in the hole" that you can play at any time, which keeps your marketing converting at an even higher level.

> **Author Note - Marketing Local Businesses**
>
> Ironically, local business marketing is both easier and harder than national level marketing. It's easier to get to work, but harder to keep working or scale. And the reason is - in local markets, it's easier because there' is trust in the familiar. So selling in- person at higher prices in a local market is inherently easier. It means you will convert a much higher percentage of your leads. This makes marketing work most of the time.
>
> The downside of local marketing is that offers fatigue rapidly because there is only a limited radius that a local business can serve. To reference an earlier concept, the TAM (total addressable market) for a brick & mortar is only its immediate radius (most times). So by extension, the smaller the radius, the faster offers fatigue. This is the double-edged sword of local.
>
> Learning to rapidly variate my offers, headlines, and creative when I had my local businesses was a cornerstone skill that made my expansion to national level advertising much easier for me. So if you are in a local market, just remember you aren't going to change the value stack of your offer. You are just going to change the way it *looks* to the marketplace in your marketing.

Naming Summary

We must appropriately name our offer to attract the right avatar to our business. True to the moniker, people *do* judge a book by its cover. Half-ass naming your product or offering can ruin conversions. Don't fall victim to lazy naming. Follow the steps here to name your product or service offering and watch the same offer get 2x, 3x, or 10x the response rate. You'll believe it when you see it - I know I did.

Enhancing Your Offer Section Recap

Congrats! You figured out how to make your offer valuable, how to break your services into component parts, and how to rebundle them into a more valuable whole.

You added a guarantee to get more people to buy your offer and actually consume it so they could be more successful.

You presented it with urgency and scarcity to get more people to desire it.

And now you've named your offer so it attracts the right prospects and repels the bad ones, all while containing a big promise everyone can understand.

But we covered a lot, so I want to give you a quick breather before we forge into Book II to help you attract clients and monetize your offer.

Free Gift # 10 BONUS: Create The Perfect Name For Your Product

Naming your product properly helps your avatar know the product is for them and is valuable and will solve their problems. If you want to do this live with me, go to **Acquisition.com/training/offers** and select **"Naming Products"** to watch a short video tutorial so you can start using this in your business to make more sales ASAP. I also made a **Free Naming Formula Checklist** for you to use and reuse with your team. It also works for naming promotions. As always, it's absolutely free. Enjoy.

SECTION V
Execution

How to Make This Happen in The Real World

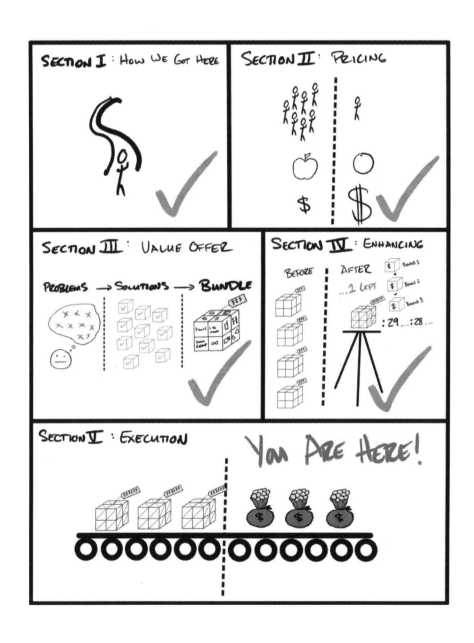

Your First $100,000

"The first $100,000 is a bitch, but you gotta do it. I don't care what you have to do—if it means walking everywhere and not eating anything that wasn't purchased with a coupon, find a way to get your hands on $100,000. After that, you can ease off the gas a little bit."

- Charlie Munger, Vice Chairman Berkshire Hathaway

March 2017.

My heart was racing. I could literally feel each beat pounding in my chest. I clenched my jaw to fend off the knot in my throat that I knew would lead to tears. I wanted to give in. Years of emotions were bottled below the surface. Years of ignoring my reality and lack of success. Years of putting off how I felt just focusing on *moving forward*. The pressure was shooting to the surface. I could *feel* it.

"We did it," I said.

Leila, my wife now, looked up at me. She was in the kitchen making dinner and stopped, spatula in hand. "What do you mean?"

"We did it. We hit $100k." I could barely get the words out because I didn't want the tears to break through the tremble in my voice.

"Like revenue?"

"No. Like in our personal bank accounts."

"Holy shit really?! That's amazing!!"

She ran over to me, disregarding the food on the stove, and wrapped her arms around my neck, spatula still in hand.

"I'm so proud of you"

She squeezed me. I slumped into her arms. It was like every knot in my body that I had been holding onto melted all at once. I could barely contain myself. But when I think back to it, the feeling I had wasn't happiness. It was relief. I'd moved from fear to security. I'd traded feeling like a failure everyday, watching my work and effort yield nothing, to realizing a dream. The constant anxiety and fear of "what are we gonna do" *finally* be replaced by something else. I finally had time to let myself feel something.

I felt like this "struggle" chapter of life was finally over.

"Look," I said. "It's for real"

I nuzzled my head out of Leila's arms. I didn't want to look her in the eyes because I knew it would put me over the edge. I pulled my phone out and put it between us. We both stared at the unmoving screen with our personal bank account balance.

$101,018

Our gazes remained unbroken as they confirmed a new, shared reality. It wasn't an illusion. It wasn't revenue. It wasn't "profit" that was still in the business account, only to be taken out later by some unforeseen emergency. It wasn't "earmarked" money that had to be used to pay off some debt. It was *ours*. For real.

"Babe," I said. "We could fuck up and not make another dollar for three straight years, and still be okay."

At the time, $33,000 per year was more than enough for us to live at our current expenses for three years *and some*.

Years of ups and downs. Years of ploughing money into my business(es) only to watch it vanish in overhead, payroll, and mistakes. Years of seminars, courses, workshops, coaching programs, masterminds . . . had F-I-N-A-L-L-Y turned into wealth. It felt like I had broken into a new plane. The relative increase in wealth was more than I ever felt.

Tens of millions of dollars in the bank later, it was, and still is, the richest I have ever felt in my life. It was the beginning of the next chapter in my life as a business person and entrepreneur.

Some people get there fast. Some people get there slowly. But everyone gets there eventually, as long as you don't give up. Keep moving forward. Keep getting up. Keep believing it can happen.

And, it will.

In A Nutshell

We've covered a lot. And I think it's important for information to sink in, that it be consolidated and restated. So this is the "back of the napkin" bullet list to summarize what we've learned so far and why.

1) We covered why you must not be a commodity in this marketplace.

2) Why you should pick a normal or growing market, and why niches get you riches.

3) Why you should charge a lot of money.

4) How to charge a lot of money using the four core value drivers.

5) How to create your value offer in five steps.

6) How to stack the value, deliver it, and make it profitable.

7) How to shift the demand curve in your favor using scarcity,

8) How to use urgency to decrease the action threshold of buyers

9) How to strategically use bonuses to increase the demand of your offer

10) How to completely reverse buyer risk with a creative guarantee.

11) How to name it in a way that resonates with your avatar.

You now have a valuable, high margin, de-commoditized grand slam offer. This is the first building block of a wonderful business — a product or service that people desperately want and truly solves their problem. For many, this will be enough to make far more sales, at higher prices, with more profit. Your first true grand slam offer should be able to get you to your first $100,000. For others, you will still want *more*. Which is 100 percent your right as a capitalist.

There's so much more to building an acquisition machine *profitably*. I could not cover it all in one book. Out of respect for you, I wanted to make this thorough but manageable. That being said, the next book is dedicated to exactly that — *getting more* — through generating leads. In that book, I will break down *exactly* how to acquire customers *at a profit*. Meaning, if you structure your promotions correctly, you should never have to pay for a new customer again. That is the subject of **Acquisition.com Volume II $100M: Lead Generation**.

Final Thoughts

Entrepreneurship is about acquiring skills, beliefs, and character traits. To advance, I find that we must determine which skills, beliefs, and character traits we *lack*. Most times, we simply need to improve. And the only way to do that is through learning from experience and/or high quality sources. I have received terrible advice from people who were ahead of me at the time. And though experience is the *best* teacher, she is not the kindest.

It is my most sincere hope that what I produce provides the guidance I so desperately needed when I was coming up on my entrepreneurial journey. And I wish I could cover it all in a single book (for my sake and yours). But, to do you the service I wish I had had, I cannot. The devil is in the details. Excellence exists in the depth of knowledge and nuances. That's what separates the greats from everyone else. I hope that in all the content I produce you see my dedication to this detail and nuance that makes *all the difference*. These lessons were hard won.

I hope you've enjoyed this first volume in my offers series. Before we move forward into volume two, where we'll be focusing on lead generation, as mentioned above, I wanted to circle back to where we started. After reading this book, I hope:

1) You're well on the path to creating your first Grand Slam Offer. Or at the very least, can take components that you were missing in your offer to make it more compelling to your market.

2) I've delivered on my promise from the beginning of this book: that investing two to three hours of your time here would yield you a far higher return than just about anything else you could do.

3) I hope in return I've taken one small step towards earning the thing I value most from you -- **your trust**.

Finally, I hope this book creates a small dent in improving the world because I believe no one is coming to save us. It's up to us, as entrepreneurs, to innovate our way into a better world. And that's something I'm willing to devote my life to. And I hope you are, too.

I'm grateful for your attention. You could have given it to anything, and you chose to invest it with me. I take it in high regard. So, sincerely, thank you.

Stay hungry,

Alex

PS - (see golden ticket below)

GOLDEN TICKET: ADMIT ONE

If you're doing $3M to $50M per year and you'd like my help 1-on-1 scaling your business go to Acquisition.com. Specifically, we help service, education, training, consulting, brick and mortar, or niche licensing companies scale *so profitably they only have to get rich once.* I'm not the "make your first dollar" person, I'm the "make the last dollar you'll ever need to make" person. If that sounds like you, you're savvy enough to figure out how to get ahold of me on my site & book a call. Would love to meet you and hear about your business and see if we can help.

Would you be opposed to growing faster? If not...

NEXT BOOK. You can check out my **next book** aptly named **Acquisition.com Volume II Lead Generation.** Which covers....lead generation. You'll never run out of new customers if you follow the steps in that book (especially now armed with the offer we have built). Not sure if that's the final name (it's still in edits), but if you search for my name, you'll find it. You'll also likely be able to find it on my site Acquisition.com (hopefully).

AUDIOBOOK. If you like listening and having all your books with you to reference (that's what I do) you can grab the **audible & kindle version of any or all my books on amazon.** I like reading and listening at the same time to increase my absorption & consumption speeds. Just search for the book titles and they'll both come up.

PODCAST. If you like listening, I have a **Podcast called "The Game"** where you can tune in to short episodes that deliver tactical lessons (learned from failures) so you can get to your goals faster. Check the podcast out here: alexspodcast.com

YOUTUBE. I have a Youtube channel with fresh tutorials a few times a week: just search my name **"Alex Hormozi"** to find it.

IG. You can follow me on IG if you like the more personal stuff: **@hormozi**